ASPIRE
SUCCEED
PROGRESS

exam success

in

ENTERPRISE

for **Cambridge IGCSE®**

Oxford excellence for Cambridge IGCSE® & O Level

OXFORD
UNIVERSITY PRESS

OXFORD
UNIVERSITY PRESS

Great Clarendon Street, Oxford, OX2 6DP, United Kingdom

Oxford University Press is a department of the University of Oxford.
It furthers the University's objective of excellence in research, scholarship, and education by publishing worldwide. Oxford is a registered trade mark of Oxford University Press in the UK and in certain other countries

British Library Cataloguing in Publication Data
Data available

978-0-19-844469-5

9 10 8

Paper used in the production of this book is a natural, recyclable product made from wood grown in sustainable forests.
The manufacturing process conforms to the environmental regulations of the country of origin.

Printed and bound by CPI Group (UK) Ltd, Croydon, CR0 4YY

Acknowledgements

The publisher and author would like to thank the following for permission to use photographs and other copyright material:

Cover: MaxxiGo/Shutterstock; **p8:** STRDEL/AFP/Getty Images; **p9:** Richard Mulonga/Newscom; **p10:** Danilo pinzon, jr/Alamy Stock Photo; **p11(t):** Zzvet/Shutterstock; **p11(m):** James Hackland/Alamy Stock Photo; **p11(b):** Foto011/Shutterstock; **p14(tl):** Asad Zaidi/Bloomberg/Getty Images; **p14(tr):** Black Star/Alamy Stock Photo; **p14(bl):** JGI/Jamie Grill/ Blend Images/Getty Images; **p14(br):** Jim West/Alamy Stock Photo; **p21:** FARJANA KHAN GODHULY/AFP/Getty Images; **p22:** Otnaydur/Shutterstock; **p23:** Monkey Business Images/Shutterstock; **p24(l):** Jake Lyell/Alamy Stock Photo; **p24(r):** Dinodia Photos/Alamy Stock Photo; **p25(t):** Dünzl/ullstein bild/Getty Images; **p25(b):** Settawat Udom/Shutterstock; **p26:** Sean Sprague/Alamy Stock Photo; **p42(t):** Jake Lyell/Alamy Stock Photo; **p42(bl):** Mboline/Fotolia; **p42(bm):** Jesse Kraft/123RF; **p42(br):** Bloomberg/Getty Images; **p46(t):** Photofusion Picture Library/Alamy Stock Photo; **p46(b):** Joerg Boethling/Alamy Stock Photo; **p47:** MS Bretherton/Alamy Stock Photo; **p51:** Yuri_Arcurs/iStockphoto; **p52:** ASDF_MEDIA/Shutterstock; **p54:** Wavebreak Media Ltd/123RF; **p75:** Janine Wiedel Photolibrary/Alamy Stock Photo; **p86:** Jerome Favre/Bloomberg/Getty Images; **p90:** Denys Prykhodov/Shutterstock; **p92:** Elizabeth Ruth Moehlmann/Moment Mobile/Getty Images; **p98:** Matej Kastelic/Shutterstock; **p99:** Getty Images; **p104:** Tatiana Koroleva/Alamy Stock Photo; **p106(t, b):** Rawpixel.com/Shutterstock; **p111:** Nyul/123RF; **p118:** Antoniodiaz/Shutterstock.

Although we have made every effort to trace and contact all copyright holders before publication this has not been possible in all cases. If notified, the publisher will rectify any errors or omissions at the earliest opportunity.

Links to third party websites are provided by Oxford in good faith and for information only. Oxford disclaims any responsibility for the materials contained in any third party website referenced in this work.

IGCSE® is the registered trademark of Cambridge Assessment International Education. All examination-style questions and answers within this publication have been written by the authors. In examination, the way marks are awarded may be different.

This Exam Success Guide refers to the Cambridge IGCSE® Enterprise (0454) Syllabus published by Cambridge Assessment International Education.

This work has been developed independently from and is not endorsed by or otherwise connected with Cambridge Assessment International Education.

The manufacturer's authorised representative in the EU for product safety is Oxford University Press España S.A. of el Parque Empresarial San Fernando de Henares, Avenida de Castilla, 2 – 28830 Madrid (www.oup.es/en).

Contents

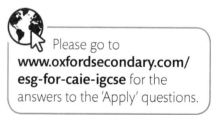
Please go to **www.oxfordsecondary.com/ esg-for-caie-igcse** for the answers to the 'Apply' questions.

Introduction

Matched to the latest Cambridge assessment criteria, this in-depth Exam Success Guide brings clarity and focus to exam preparation with detailed and practical guidance on raising attainment in IGCSE® & O Level Enterprise.

This Exam Success Guide can be used alongside *Complete Enterprise for Cambridge IGCSE®*, second edition, and contains numerous references to the Student Book.

This Exam Success Guide:

- is fully matched to the latest Cambridge IGCSE® & O Level syllabuses

- includes comprehensive **Recap** and **Review** features that focus on key course content

- equips you to **Raise your grade** with sample responses and examiner commentary

- will help you to avoid mistakes with **Common error** tips

- will help you to understand exam expectations with **Exam tips**

- equips you to test knowledge via **Apply** questions, and provides answers online at www.oxfordsecondary.com/esg-for-caie-igcse

- provides you with a **Revision checklist** for each unit, which will enable you to build a record of your revision

- is perfect for use alongside the *Complete Enterprise for Cambridge IGCSE®*, second edition, or as a standalone resource for independent revision.

Key revision points are included as follows:

- **You need to know:** at the start of every section. This summarises the key things you need to know for each topic.

- **Key terms:** definitions of the key terms and concepts. These are given the first time the term is used in the book and they also appear in the **Glossary**.

- **Exam tips:** these tips give clear details on how to maximise marks in the exam.

- **Common errors:** these give an indication of areas of the syllabus where students commonly struggle. By looking closely at these, you should avoid making similar mistakes in your exam.

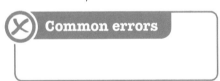

- **Recap:** each section of the book recaps the key content through easy-to-digest chunks.

- **Apply:** these provide targeted exam-style questions for you to answer. They have been written specifically for this Exam Success Guide and will help you to apply your knowledge and understanding in the exam. Answers to these questions are available online.

- **Review:** throughout each section of the book, you can review and reflect on the work you have done and find advice and guidance on how to further refresh and deepen your knowledge and understanding. This will include references to the Student Book.

- **Raise your grade:** these sections can be found at the end of each unit. They include exam-style sample questions, an analysis of these questions, the mark scheme and an example student answer. Examiner feedback indicates why a particular mark was awarded and gives advice on how the answer could have been improved to gain a higher mark.

- **Revision checklist:** these checklists appear at the start of each unit. They will enable you to record your revision.

- **Coursework tips:** these tips give clear advice and guidance on what you will need to do in your coursework.

How will you be assessed?

All candidates take two papers for their IGCSE® or O Level Enterprise exam, Component 1 and Component 2.

Component 1: Written Paper (1 hour 30 minutes)

This component consists of short-answer, structured and open-ended questions. It is based on a pre-released case study. Candidates answer all questions. Component 1 is externally assessed. This paper carries 100 marks and these represent 50% of the total marks.

Component 2: Coursework

Candidates need to submit a portfolio of evidence from tasks based on the their own enterprise project. Component 2 is internally assessed and externally moderated. This paper carries 60 marks and these represent 50% of the total marks.

Assessment objectives

There are three assessment objectives (AOs). These are:

- knowledge and understanding (AO1)

- application (AO2)

- analysis and evaluation (AO3).

Knowledge and understanding

You should be able to:

- demonstrate knowledge and understanding of the concepts, skills and terminology related to enterprise.

Application

You should be able to:

- apply knowledge and critical understanding to familiar and unfamiliar enterprise problems and issues

- develop communication materials appropriate for the intended audience and purpose.

Analysis and evaluation

You should be able to:

- analyse, interpret and evaluate information
- explore and find solutions to enterprise problems and issues.

Assessment structure

Assessment Objective	Component 1 (50%)	Component 2 (50%)
AO1 Knowledge and understanding	38	10
AO2 Application	30	35
AO3 Analysis and evaluation	32	55

The value of studying Enterprise

This course will encourage you to develop your knowledge and understanding of Enterprise and your ability to use practical skills associated with the work environment. You will gain an awareness of what is involved in running a small enterprise and you will have an opportunity to apply this knowledge and understanding in a practical and engaging way when running your own enterprise project.

The course will provide you with opportunities to meet with, and talk to, a range of people involved in the world of enterprise, including:

- people who have set up and run their own enterprises
- people who are, or have been, involved in supporting enterprises, such as financiers, local business organisations and government organisations
- people who have demonstrated enterprising skills, such as innovators, inventors and marketing professionals.

The Enterprise course has a number of aims that will enable you to:

- understand what it means to be enterprising
- understand the skills required to be enterprising
- develop the ability to work in an enterprising, creative and independent way
- develop and apply knowledge, understanding and skills to contemporary enterprise issues in a range of local, regional, national and global contexts
- appreciate the roles and perspectives of a number of other people and organisations involved in enterprise
- understand the importance of ethical considerations
- investigate the world of work and entrepreneurial organisations
- develop the ability to communicate effectively, in a variety of situations, using a range of appropriate techniques
- make effective use of relevant terms, concepts and methods when discussing enterprise and enterprising behaviour.

Enterprise skills can be important in helping you to succeed in your further and higher education studies. Throughout this course, you will develop skills of critical thinking, problem-solving, communication, risk-taking, teamwork and decision-making.

It is also important that you are equipped with the skills necessary to succeed in the world of work. You will need to be innovative, adaptable, resilient and flexible, and Enterprise has never been more important in this respect. Enterprise skills will enhance your employability.

Unit 1:
Introduction to enterprise

Your exam

Introduction to enterprise is part of Component 1: Written Paper, and Component 2: Coursework.

Component 1 is a 90-minute exam and makes up 50% of the total marks.
Component 2 is the coursework and makes up 50% of the total marks.

Your revision checklist

Tick these boxes to build a record of your revision

Specification	Theme	Tick
1.1 What is meant by enterprise?	What enterprise is	
	Who stakeholders are	
1.2 Ways for students to be enterprising in everyday life	Ways of being enterprising at school	
	Ways of being enterprising at home	

You need to know:

- about enterprise capability (being innovative, creative, taking and managing risks, positive attitude)
- about business enterprise and social enterprise
- examples of stakeholders.

Key terms

Business enterprise: a type of enterprise that usually has profit as its main objective

Creative: the ability to introduce something original and imaginative

Dividend: a share of the profit of an enterprise in the form of a payment to its shareholders

Enterprise: a business organised and run by an entrepreneur

Entrepreneur: the person in an enterprise who makes decisions and takes and manages risks

Innovate: the ability to introduce something new or different

Positive attitude: the tendency to be optimistic

Risk: the possibility that events in relation to an enterprise do not turn out as expected

What enterprise is

Enterprise capability

Enterprise capability involves a number of key aspects.

Aspect	Explanation
Being innovative	This includes coming up with new ideas and products, challenging traditional approaches and finding new ways to solve problems.
Being creative	This includes the process of turning new and imaginative ideas into reality. Creativity involves the ability to see the world in new ways and to generate appropriate solutions.
Taking and managing risks	Decision-making in enterprise involves taking a risk – one of the key characteristics of enterprise. The entrepreneur is the person responsible for taking a risk and for managing that risk in an appropriate way.
Having a positive attitude	This involves optimism and the willingness and ability to motivate all those involved with an enterprise to strive for success. A positive attitude encourages constructive and imaginative thinking and the desire to accomplish goals. It makes an entrepreneur more resilient and more likely to make better decisions.

Business enterprise

A business enterprise is usually one that provides goods and services with the aim of making money, i.e. it is expected that a profit will be made as a result of the business enterprise activity. The profit will then be retained and reinvested into the enterprise or distributed to its owners in the form of a dividend.

▲ **Figure 1** *A design enterprise that aims to make a profit is an example of a business enterprise*

Social enterprise

Whereas a business enterprise usually aims to make a profit, a social enterprise does not have such an aim and is usually a not-for-profit organisation. It aims for the improvement of society in some way and if a profit is made, it is usually reinvested into the community.

▲ **Figure 2** *A sports enterprise that does not aim to make a profit is an example of a social enterprise*

Who stakeholders are

A stakeholder is a person, group or organisation with an interest or concern in something, such as an enterprise. The stakeholders can affect, and/or be affected by, the enterprise's actions, objectives and policies – this impact can be positive or negative.

The following are the different kinds of stakeholder involved in an enterprise.

Customers and consumers

- Customers buy goods and services generating income for the enterprise.

- Enterprises must understand the needs and wants of their customers. If enterprises produce products that are not demanded by customers, they are likely to go out of business.

- Consumers have increasing rights and protection so most enterprises work very hard at promoting good customer relations.

Employees and employers

- Employees are employed by an enterprise to help its activity in some way.

- An enterprise needs employees with a range of skills and knowledge and many will provide training to new employees to familiarise them with its policies and working practices.

- The managers of an enterprise can usually be regarded as employees. If an enterprise is operated by the owner, the owner can be regarded as the employer.

 Key term

Social enterprise: a type of enterprise that does not usually have profit as its main objective

 Common error

Candidates sometimes confuse a business enterprise and a social enterprise. Make sure you clearly understand the difference between these two types of enterprise.

Exam tip

When answering questions about the meaning of the term 'enterprise', make sure you understand that not all enterprises exist to make a profit. Some are not-for-profit organisations.

 Coursework tip

You will need to decide whether your coursework project is going to be a business enterprise or a social enterprise.

 Coursework tip

You will need to identify and explain the role of the stakeholders who will be involved in your coursework enterprise.

Suppliers

- Suppliers provide the resources, such as raw materials, energy, component parts, tools and equipment that allow enterprises to produce goods and services.
- Enterprises and suppliers rely on each other so they must have a good relationship:
  - Suppliers must provide quality resources at reasonable prices with a reliable and flexible service
  - Enterprises need to provide a constant flow of orders and pay on time.

Lenders

- Many enterprises may need to borrow funds from a financial institution to stay in business or to finance expansion. As a result, there needs to be a good relationship between an enterprise (the borrower) and a financial institution (the lender):
- Enterprises need to know that they can go to a financial institution to borrow money if that becomes necessary.
- On their part, financial institutions need to know that they will get this money back from an enterprise, plus any interest that has been charged on the loan.

The local business community

- Enterprises will employ local people so good relationships are likely to exist with the local business community.
- An enterprise may also need input from local businesses in the form of training, such as information about courses provided by local colleges and universities.
- Enterprises can also become involved in community life through the sponsorship of local sports teams or through local charity fund raising.

Local government

- Enterprises may have to work closely with local government agencies.
- This could include, for example, planning applications, and the payment of taxes to local government.

▲ **Figure 3** *Customers and consumers are stakeholders in an enterprise*

▲ **Figure 4** *Employees are stakeholders in an enterprise*

▲ **Figure 5** *Suppliers are stakeholders in an enterprise*

▲ **Figure 6** *The local business community is a stakeholder in an enterprise*

🔑 Key terms

Customer: a person or organisation that buys goods and/or services from an enterprise

Stakeholders: various groups with a strong interest in a particular enterprise, including customers and consumers, employees and employers, suppliers, lenders, the local business community and local government

Suppliers: businesses providing resources to an enterprise that allows it to produce goods and services

Exam tip

You need to be able to refer to a variety of different stakeholders in an enterprise.

Make sure you understand that not all stakeholders in an enterprise may be equally important.

⊗ Common error

Candidates are usually able to describe what is meant by a stakeholder, but they are not always able to give appropriate examples of stakeholders.

Recap

- Enterprise capability involves the combination of being innovative, being creative, taking and managing risks and having a positive attitude.

- A business enterprise usually has profit as its main objective.

- A social enterprise is usually a not-for-profit organisation.

- Examples of stakeholders include:

  - customers and consumers

  - employees and employers

  - suppliers

  - lenders

  - the local business community

  - local government.

Apply

1. Explain what is meant by 'enterprise capability'.

2. Distinguish between a business enterprise and a social enterprise.

3. Explain, with the use of examples, what is meant by a stakeholder in an enterprise.

Review

It is important to understand that an enterprise should have good relationships with its stakeholders, such as customers, employees, suppliers and the local community.

These stakeholders can have a positive impact on the work of an enterprise, making it more likely that it will be able to expand its customer base and be successful, e.g. make a profit.

The legal implications of these relationships will be considered in section 4.3.

You need to know:

- ways of being enterprising at school; technology, teamwork, evaluation, developing new skills, initiative, problem-solving

- ways of being enterprising at home; organising household jobs, taking responsibility for children and pets, earning money.

Ways of being enterprising at school

Ways of being enterprising	Explanation
Using technology for learning	• Technology can be used for learning, both inside and outside of school. For example, a student could be enterprising by researching a number of different sources, using the internet as a learning tool.
Working or learning as part of a team	• It is important to be able to work as part of a team. Teamwork is stressed in many group activities at school, while at home, learning will often be as part of a wider social group, i.e. the family.
	• Schools may organise specific days, or even a week, that focus on being enterprising, where guest speakers are invited to give a talk. Students are given the opportunity to work together in teams and to come up with possible enterprise opportunities.
Making reasoned evaluations	• Evaluation is a key part of being enterprising, and involves comparing different options before coming to a conclusion that is reasoned, logical and justifiable.
Developing new skills and using them in different situations	• Critical thinking means going outside the established ways of approaching a problem and involves the idea of 'thinking smarter'. This should lead to improved problem-solving and decision-making. Applying critical thinking to new contexts is an important part of being enterprising.
	• Written and non-written communication skills, as well as numeracy skills, should be developed in order to be enterprising. Being enterprising involves applying learning to new situations that are not familiar – out of the 'comfort zone'. Many important skills needed in enterprise are transferable, i.e. they can be used in different situations and contexts.
Problem-solving	• The ability to solve problems is an important part of being enterprising. Many people see a problem (both at school and at home) as a challenge to be overcome and so approach it in a positive and imaginative way.
	• A student could be enterprising in looking at a particular problem from different perspectives.
Thinking creatively	• To be enterprising, it is often important to think creatively about different ways to approach and solve a problem and to come up with new ideas or new approaches. This can be important in a school context.
	• Entrepreneurs are often very creative people who are willing to think independently to go beyond traditional methods to achieve their objective.
	• A student could be enterprising in terms of thinking critically and creatively about a particular topic or theme, such as in literature or in art – thinking 'outside of the box'.
Taking the initiative or taking the lead	• An important feature of being enterprising is the ability and willingness to take the initiative – being a leader. This could be rewarded at school by, for example, being made a prefect.
Organising activities	• Being involved in the organisation of an event to raise money for a charity will give students valuable experience of what is involved in the organisation of an enterprise.

 **Key term**

Enterprising: the showing of initiative, imagination, energy and resourcefulness

▲ **Figure 7** *Using technology for learning*

▲ **Figure 8** *A guest speaker at a school Enterprise Day*

Ways of being enterprising at home

Ways of being enterprising	Explanation
Organising a household job	• You can be enterprising by offering to do jobs at home, e.g. helping with the shopping, and household cleaning and cooking.
Taking responsibility for younger children	• You can be enterprising at home by looking after younger brothers or sisters. This demonstrates maturity and responsibility for your actions.
Taking responsibility for pets	• If you have a family pet, you could demonstrate responsibility by taking on the tasks that ensure its wellbeing.
Earning money for the family	• You might be able to bring money into the family by being enterprising, e.g. by charging a small fee for doing shopping for older or disabled people.

▲ **Figure 9** *Being enterprising at home in the kitchen*

▲ **Figure 10** *Being enterprising at home in the garden*

Recap

- There are many different ways of being enterprising at school, such as using technology for learning, working and learning as part of a team, making reasoned evaluations, developing new skills and using them in different situations, problem-solving, thinking creatively, taking the initiative or taking the lead and organising activities.

- There are many different ways of being enterprising at home, such as organising a household job, taking responsibility for younger children, taking responsibility for pets and earning money for the family.

 Coursework tip

You will need to think about the different ways that you can be enterprising in order to make a positive contribution to your enterprise project.

 Apply

1. Describe how technology for learning can be used as an example of being enterprising at school.

2. Describe **one** way that you have been enterprising at home.

 Review

Some of the ways of being enterprising at school can also be applied to being enterprising at home, such as working and learning as part of a team, developing new skills and using them in different situations, and problem-solving.

Sample question

1. **a.** Define the term 'entrepreneur'. [2]

   b. Explain why having a positive attitude is a key aspect of enterprise capability. [4]

   c. Explain **two** reasons why the relationship between an enterprise and its suppliers needs to be a good one. [6]

   d. Analyse why taking the initiative, either at school or at home, is regarded as a good example of being enterprising. [10]

Analysis

✓ In (a), you will need to clearly define what is meant by the term 'entrepreneur'.

✓ In (b), you will need to focus on providing an explanation of why a positive attitude is regarded as an important aspect of enterprise capability.

✓ In (c), you will need to clearly explain two reasons why an enterprise and its suppliers need to have a very good relationship.

✓ In (d), you will need to analyse, and not simply describe, why taking the initiative is regarded as a good example of being enterprising. Your answer can be in the context of either school or home.

Mark scheme

a. One mark for stating that an entrepreneur is the person in an enterprise who makes decisions; one mark for stating that an entrepreneur is the person in an enterprise who takes and manages risks.

b. Up to four marks for an explanation that focuses on: optimism and the willingness and ability to motivate all those involved with an enterprise to strive for success; the encouragement of constructive and imaginative thinking and the desire to accomplish goals; the possibility of making an entrepreneur more resilient and more likely to make better decisions.

c. Up to three marks for an explanation of each of two reasons why the relationship between an enterprise and its suppliers needs to be a good one. Reasons could include: the fact that suppliers provide the resources that allow enterprises to produce goods and services; the fact that enterprises require suppliers to provide quality resources at reasonable prices; the fact that enterprises require suppliers to provide a reliable and flexible service; the fact that suppliers require enterprises to provide a constant flow of orders and to pay on time.

d. Knowledge and understanding, Level 1, 1–3 marks; some analysis, Level 2, 4–7 marks; good analysis, Level 3, 8–10 marks.

Student answer

(a) An entrepreneur is the person in an enterprise who takes the most significant decisions.

[1 mark]

(b) It is important to have a positive attitude in enterprise because this will help to make a person optimistic and enthusiastic. This will contribute to others in the enterprise being well-motivated, so that the enterprise is more likely to be a success. [2 marks]

(c) One reason why the relationship between an enterprise and its suppliers needs to be a good one is that the enterprise will be able to obtain all the resources that it needs at the right time and at the right price. A second reason is that the suppliers need the enterprise to be a consistent and reliable source of orders. [3 marks]

(d) Being enterprising is a key part of enterprise capability and one element of being enterprising is the ability and willingness to take the initiative. This will often involve people leading others, and this is important in the school situation. Many people at school who are willing to take the initiative and lead others are rewarded in an appropriate way, e.g. by being made a prefect or even a head boy or head girl. Effective leadership is important to the success of an enterprise and a school is likely to provide a range of opportunities for the demonstration of leadership qualities by taking the initiative.

[4 marks]

Total: 10 out of 22

✓ Examiner feedback

a. The candidate has referred to an entrepreneur being the person in an enterprise who takes the most difficult decisions, but there is no reference to the fact that an entrepreneur is the person in an enterprise who takes and manages risks.

b. The candidate has made a reasonable attempt to explain why having a positive attitude is a key aspect of enterprise capability, but the answer could have been developed more fully. For example, there could have been more of an emphasis on striving for success and on constructive and imaginative thinking in relation to achieving goals. There could also have been a reference to resilience and to the link with better decision-making..

c. The candidate has made quite a good attempt to explain two reasons why the relationship between enterprises and suppliers needs to be a good one, but each of the reasons given could have been explained more fully. In terms of the first one, the candidate could have given some examples of possible resources, such as raw materials, component parts, tools and equipment, energy and a variety of different services. The references to 'the right time' and to 'the right price' were rather

brief and could have gone further, e.g. a reference to a price that was agreeable to both the enterprise and the supplier. In terms of the second reason, the explanation could have been developed in relation to the need of the supplier to receive payment on time so as to avoid any cash flow problems.

d. The candidate clearly recognises the importance of taking the initiative in the context of enterprise and makes some useful comments about the possibilities of exercising leadership in a school, such as being the head boy or head girl. However, the analysis needed to go further in relation to taking the initiative being an example of enterprising. For example, the candidate could have referred to a person taking the initiative by becoming the captain of a sports team, leading a school club or helping to set up and establish a project or campaign, such as one linked with a charity event or with improving the school environment. Also, there needed to have been more of a focus on the link with enterprise, e.g. the idea of taking the initiative by being bold and imaginative in the enterprise context, such as in recognising a gap in a market.

Unit 2:
Setting up a new enterprise

Your exam

Setting up a new enterprise is part of Component 1: Written Paper, and Component 2: Coursework.

Component 1 is a 90-minute exam and makes up 50% of the total marks.
Component 2 is the coursework and makes up 50% of the total marks.

Your revision checklist

Tick these boxes to build a record of your revision

Specification	Theme	Tick
2.1 The enterprise process	The six stages of the enterprise process	
2.2 Types of business organisation	Sole trader	
	Partnership	
	Limited company	
	Co-operative	
	Franchise	
	Social enterprise	

- the six stages of the enterprise process.

The six stages of the enterprise process

It is possible to differentiate between six stages of the enterprise process.

> **1. Identifying the problem or need or want.**
> The problem or need or want needs to be identified before a solution can be found.

> **2. Exploring creative solutions.**
> These solutions may require creative and imaginative approaches with an enterprise having to go 'outside of the box'.

> **3. Action planning.**
> Action planning helps to focus ideas and to decide and prioritise the steps that need to be taken to achieve the goals of an enterprise.

> **4. Implementing the plan.**
> An effective action plan will provide a clear timetable and a set of clearly defined steps to help to reach the objectives.

> **5. Monitoring progress.**
> Monitoring progress to judge how well the plan is being implemented and how well the objectives are being achieved.

> **6. Evaluation of successes and failures.**
> Evaluation will identify the factors that affected the success or failure of a plan, which will enable recommendations for improvements to be made.

 **Key terms**

Action plan: a plan that outlines the actions required to achieve particular aims and objectives and which provides a way of monitoring progress

Enterprise process: the six stages that are involved in the setting up of a new enterprise

It is important that you clearly understand each of the six stages of the enterprise process. For example, in terms of stage 5, monitoring progress, the following questions need to be asked:

- Has each step of the plan been implemented correctly?

- Has each step of the plan been implemented on time?

- Has the expected outcome materialised from the completion of each step?

Common error

Candidates sometimes confuse monitoring progress and the evaluation of successes and failures. Make sure you clearly understand the difference between the fifth and sixth stages of the enterprise process.

Exam tip

Monitoring the progress of a plan should not be confused with its evaluation. Monitoring a plan helps to ensure that the solution is being implemented as expected. Evaluating the solution occurs after the plan has been implemented and provides an indication of the successes and failures of the plan.

Coursework tip

You need to follow the six stages of the enterprise process when working on your enterprise project in Component 2: Coursework.

The following additional questions may need to be asked, based on the answers to the previous questions:

- Is more time required?
- Are more tasks required?
- Are more resources required?
- Was the plan realistic?
- What action needs to be taken?
- Does the plan need to change?

 Recap

There are six stages of the enterprise process:

- identifying the problem or need or want
- exploring creative solutions
- action planning
- implementing the plan
- monitoring progress
- evaluating successes and failures.

Apply

Explain why exploring creative solutions is an important stage in the enterprise process.

Review

You must understand exactly what is involved in the six stages of the enterprise process – from the identification of the problem or need or want, to the evaluation of successes or failures – in order to give a clear indication of what is involved in the setting up of a new enterprise.

A clear understanding of how these stages follow each other and link together is important in having an awareness and an appreciation of what the enterprise process is all about and what it is trying to achieve.

You need to know:
- the legal status of a sole trader, partnership, limited company, co-operative, franchise and social enterprise
- the advantages and disadvantages of each of the above.

Sole trader

Sole traders are people who run their own (usually) relatively small enterprise themselves, although they may employ a number of people. The legal status of a sole trader enterprise is that it is an unincorporated enterprise, i.e. it is not a separate legal entity from the owner.

▲ **Figure 1** *An example of an enterprise organised as a sole trader*

Advantages and disadvantages of a sole trader for a new enterprise

Advantages	Disadvantages
Sole trader enterprises are relatively simple to establish and there is usually no need to obtain special legal documents.	There is unlimited liability – the owner is responsible for debts and can be forced to sell personal possessions to pay them.
The sole trader (owner) can take decisions independently and so have complete control of the enterprise.	There may be difficulties in raising finance, e.g. sole traders are less likely to be loaned money than larger enterprises as they are more likely to go bankrupt.
Any profit made after tax can be kept by the owner.	The owner may lack the skills or experience to make the key decisions.
There is usually no legal requirement to publish accounts.	It may be difficult to compete with larger firms, e.g. a larger firm can negotiate discounts because it buys in larger quantities.
There can be greater flexibility in the hours of work.	The enterprise is an unincorporated business, the owner can be personally taken to court if there is a dispute.
Sole traders can usually provide a more personal service to customers.	All the responsibility for taking day-to-day enterprise decisions is in the hands of the owner.
In some countries, sole traders may receive financial support from the government.	The life of the business is limited.

Exam tip

Make sure you fully understand the implications of unlimited liability for sole traders.

 Key terms

Business organisation: an organisation that has been established with the purpose of producing and selling particular goods and services

Sole trader: a person responsible for setting up and running an enterprise that he or she runs alone

Unincorporated enterprise: an enterprise that does not have a separate legal identity from the owner

Unlimited liability: the need for sole traders and partners (except limited partners) to pay the debts of an enterprise out of their own personal funds

 Common error

It is sometimes thought that a sole trader refers to an enterprise in which one person is working alone. This is, of course, possible, but a sole trader will often employ a number of people. The key point to stress is that the sole trader is the one person who legally owns the enterprise.

▲ **Figure 2** *Two of the partners in a partnership*

Exam tip

Make sure you understand that sole trader and partnership types of business organisation have the same legal status in that both are unincorporated enterprises with the owners having unlimited liability.

 Key terms

Incorporated enterprise: an enterprise that has a separate legal identity from the owner

Limited company: a company that is legally independent from its shareholders, who as a result have limited liability

Limited liability: legal protection that allows shareholders to be liable for company debts only up to the value of their shareholding

Partnership: a type of business organisation that is owned by two or more people

Partnership

A partnership is a type of business organisation owned by two or more people, with a maximum of 20 in many countries. The legal status of this type of business organisation is the same as that of a sole trader: it is unincorporated and, as a result, the partners have unlimited liability.

Advantages and disadvantages of a partnership for a new enterprise

Advantages	Disadvantages
Partnerships are relatively easy to form. They usually require a legal contract, signed by all partners, called a deed of partnership.	Ordinary partners have unlimited liability and may be asked to sell personal possessions if the partnership gets into debt, although in some countries it is possible to be a limited partner, i.e. someone with limited liability.
Having more than one owner makes it easier to raise money compared with a sole trader (but a partnership will be able to raise less money than a limited company).	Any decision made by one partner is legally binding on all of the partners.
There is usually no need to publicly disclose a partnership's accounts.	Disagreements between partners can make decision-making difficult.
A partnership may be able to negotiate discounts with suppliers, gaining cost advantages known as economies of scale.	A partnership may not be large enough to gain economies of scale, preventing it from substantially reducing its costs.
Partners can specialise in particular aspects of the work.	If one of the partners leaves or dies, the partnership is dissolved.
The partners keep all the profits, i.e. there are no shareholders to share them with.	Profits have to be shared among all the partners.
Partners are in charge of the enterprise and can share the decision-making and the workload.	Like sole traders, partners can be sued by customers.

Limited company

A limited company is an unincorporated enterprise, i.e. it is a separate legal entity from the owners. This means that there is limited liability, so people who put money into a limited company can only lose this money if the company goes bankrupt; their own personal possessions are not at risk.

There are private and public limited companies. The shares of a private limited company cannot be bought by members of the public and a minimum and maximum number of shareholders is often set. The shares of a public limited company are sold on a stock exchange and they can be bought by members of the general public.

There is usually a minimum amount of capital required to establish a public limited company.

Advantages and disadvantages of a limited company for a new enterprise

Advantages	Disadvantages
Limited companies can usually raise more money than sole traders or partnerships. Setting up a limited company (especially a public limited company) is particularly appropriate if the enterprise plans to become large.	The accounts of a limited company must be made available to the public.
	The original founders of the company may lose control as members of the public buy shares.
	A minimum amount of capital is needed to establish a limited company.
Shareholders have limited liability, i.e. they cannot lose their personal possessions if the company goes bankrupt.	Profits have to be shared out among a large number of people.
	Shares of a private limited company cannot be sold to the general public. This can limit the amount of capital that can be raised.
Limited companies are usually able to gain economies of scale, leading to a fall in the costs of production.	There is often a divorce or separation of ownership and control.
	Owing to their large size, limited companies may be inflexible.
A limited company will continue even if one of the owners dies.	They are not as easy to set up as a sole trader or a partnership as there are many legal formalities to go through before a company can be established.

Co-operative

There are two main types of co-operative:

- *A consumer or retail co-operative* is owned by its members. These are members of the public, many of whom regularly use the co-operative who buy shares, but they are usually limited to one vote at shareholder meetings, no matter how many shares they have. The profit is not usually distributed to shareholders, but to the shoppers who use the co-operative.

- *A producer or worker co-operative* is owned by some or all of the workers in a particular firm. The profit is usually distributed to the workers, who are its shareholders. Examples can be found in many different kinds of agricultural activities in many countries, such as where farmers come together in a particular area to control the production and distribution of produce.

Other types of co-operative, e.g. in banking and insurance, exist in some countries.

Exam tip

Make sure you understand the differences in legal status between sole traders, partnerships, and limited companies.

Exam tip

Make sure you understand the similarities and differences between a private limited company and a public limited company.

▲ **Figure 3** *A meeting in a limited company*

Co-operative: a type of business organisation owned by its customers or its employees

Exam tip

Make sure you are able to distinguish clearly between consumer and producer co-operatives.

Advantages and disadvantages of a co-operative for a new enterprise

Advantages	Disadvantages
Shareholders in a consumer or producer co-operative usually have limited liability.	Shares in a co-operative are not usually sold on a stock exchange and this can limit the amount of capital that can be raised.
In a producer co-operative, the workers are the shareholders, so they are less likely to be involved in disputes and more likely to be well motivated and to work hard.	In a producer co-operative, the workers can find it difficult to raise enough capital to set up a new enterprise.
There is usually democratic ownership, on the basis of one member, one vote, and many co-operatives are keen to be involved in the local community and may be more ethical than other enterprises.	In a producer co-operative, the workers often lack the necessary experience and skills to make the enterprise successful, so they have to appoint managers.
In a consumer co-operative, the enterprise is run in the customers' interests.	The need to employ managers to run a co-operative is expensive.
Most co-operatives are a distinct legal entity and so the death of one member does not alter its continued existence.	The accounts have to be made available to the public.

▲ **Figure 4** *An enterprise organised as a co-operative*

▲ **Figure 5** *The milk silos of the Amul Dairy Co-operative in India*

Franchise

A franchise arrangement allows an enterprise to purchase the right to sell a particular product. The enterprise, known as the franchisee, makes a payment to the owner of an established branded product, known as the franchisor. The franchisee can then sell the product and take advantage of the marketing provided by the franchisor.

Five of the most famous franchises in the world are McDonald's, The Body Shop, Burger King, Pizza Hut and Subway.

Advantages and disadvantages of a franchise for a new enterprise

Advantages	Disadvantages
The franchisee is able to sell a well-known and recognised branded product and so the revenue received is likely to be significant.	The franchisee will need to make a payment to the franchisor for the franchise rights. This will usually still have to be made even if the franchisee makes a loss.
Some of the advertising will be carried out by the franchisor, keeping down the costs of advertising by the franchisee.	In addition to the initial fee, the franchisee will usually be required to pay a percentage of the sales revenue to the franchisor every year.
A franchise arrangement is likely to be less risky than starting up an enterprise with a new name because the branded product will be familiar to many people and so there is likely to be less risk of failure.	The franchisor may strictly control the activities of the franchisee, such as the design of the premises, the use of suppliers and possibly the area of operation. This can be regarded as very restrictive by the franchisee.
Certain services, such as training and some aspects of administration, may be carried out by the franchisor, saving the franchisee money.	The franchisor has the power to withdraw the agreement and sometimes can prevent the franchisee from using the premises.
It is likely to be easier to obtain funds from financial institutions as the enterprise is likely to be seen as relatively low risk.	The initial costs of setting up a franchise are likely to be quite high.

Social enterprise

Like any other enterprise, social enterprises make their money from selling goods and services in a market, but they then reinvest their profits into the local community. They therefore have the maximisation of social impact as their main objective rather than the maximisation of profit.

A charity is an example of a social enterprise. Charities raise money for a 'good cause', relying on donations and fundraising events for revenue. Some also run business enterprises, e.g. shops. In many countries registered charities do not pay tax.

A social enterprise is often a not-for-profit organisation. A profit may be made, but it is then reinvested into the organisation. Some schools, colleges and hospitals are not-for-profit organisations. The emphasis is on social and ethical responsibility. Unlike a charity, a not-for-profit organisation does not rely on donations.

 Common error

A franchisee and a franchisor are sometimes confused, so make sure you clearly understand the difference between these two terms.

▲ **Figure 6** *An example of a franchise enterprise*

▲ **Figure 7** *An example of a franchise enterprise*

Exam tip

You need to understand that if charitable organisations bring in more money than they spend, this is not recorded as a profit but as a surplus.

Although charities and not-for-profit organisations are both examples of a social enterprise, they are not the same. For example, charities usually rely heavily on donations, but not-for-profit organisations do not.

Exam tip

Make sure you are able to explain how a social enterprise differs from other types of business organisation.

Advantages and disadvantages of a social enterprise organisation for a new enterprise

Advantages	Disadvantages
The people who work for a social enterprise usually have a strong interest in the aims and objectives of the enterprise.	It may be relatively difficult to obtain the capital that is needed to adequately finance the organisation.
The level of job satisfaction and motivation is likely to be relatively high.	The organisation may be less competitive in a market because of the absence of a profit motive.
The workers in a social enterprise are generally committed to bringing about an improvement in the community.	It is possible that because of the lack of a profit motive, the organisation is not as efficient as it could be.

There are six different types of business organisation:

- sole trader
- partnership
- limited company
- co-operative
- franchise
- social enterprise.

▲ **Figure 8** *Staff from a social enterprise at work*

Exam tip

You will not be assessed on limited liability partnerships or community interest companies.

Apply

1. Explain **two** advantages and **two** disadvantages of a sole trader as a business organisation for a new enterprise.

2. Describe the main features of a social enterprise.

Review

It is important that you recognise not only the features and characteristics of the different types of business organisation, but also the advantages and disadvantages of each of them, specifically for a new enterprise.

To help you to understand the distinctive features and characteristics of a business organisation, see the case studies in the Student Book of the Amul Dairy Co-operative on page 34, the Subway franchise on page 36 and the Re-Cycle (Bikes to Africa) social enterprise on page 37.

Sample question

1. **a.** Define the term 'action plan'. **[2]**

    b. Explain why it is important for an enterprise to monitor the progress of its action plan. **[4]**

    c. Describe **two** advantages and **two** disadvantages of a limited company as a business organisation for a new enterprise. **[8]**

    d. Discuss whether a franchise would be the best type of business organisation for a new enterprise. **[15]**

Analysis

✓ In (a), you will need to clearly define what is meant by the term 'action plan'.

✓ In (b), you will need to focus on providing an explanation of why it is important for an enterprise to monitor the progress of its action plan.

✓ In (c), you will need to accurately describe two advantages and two disadvantages of a limited company as a business organisation for a new enterprise.

✓ In (d), you will need to discuss whether a franchise would be the best type of business organisation for a new enterprise, comparing and contrasting the various advantages and disadvantages of such an arrangement.

Mark scheme

a. One mark for stating that an action plan outlines the actions required to achieve particular aims and objectives; one mark for stating that an action plan provides a way of monitoring the progress of an enterprise.

b. Up to four marks for an explanation of why it is important for an enterprise to monitor the progress of its action plan, in terms of judging how well the aims and objectives are being achieved, i.e. how well the plan is functioning.

c. Up to two marks for each of two descriptions of the advantages of a limited company as a business organisation for a new enterprise. For example, limited companies can usually raise more money than sole traders or partnerships; or shareholders have limited liability and cannot lose their personal possessions if the company goes bankrupt; or limited companies are usually able to gain economies of scale; or a limited company will continue even if one of the owners dies. Up to two marks for each of two descriptions of the possible disadvantages. For example, the accounts of a limited company must be made available to the public; or the original founders may lose control as people buy shares; or a minimum amount of capital is needed to establish a limited company; or profits have to be shared out among a large number of people; or shares of a private limited company cannot be sold to the general public; or there is often a divorce of ownership.

d. Knowledge and understanding, Level 1, 1–3 marks; some analysis, Level 2, 4–7 marks; good analysis, Level 3, 8–11 marks; clear reasoned evaluation, Level 4, 12–15 marks.

Student answer

(a) An action plan is used by an enterprise as a way of outlining the various actions required to achieve the particular aims and objectives of the enterprise. [1 mark]

(b) The monitoring of progress to judge how well an action plan is being implemented is the fifth stage of the enterprise process. It is important because it enables a judgment to be made about how well the aims and objectives of the plan are being achieved. Monitoring the progress of the action plan helps to ensure that it is being implemented successfully. As part of this process of monitoring, there are a number of key questions that can and should be asked, such as has each step of the plan been implemented correctly, has each step of the plan been implemented on time, and has the expected outcome come about from the completion of each step? [4 marks]

(c) One advantage of a limited company as a business organisation for a new enterprise is that limited companies can usually raise more money than sole traders or partnerships. This applies especially to a public limited company as shares can be issued to the general public through a stock exchange, which is particularly appropriate if the enterprise plans to become large. One disadvantage is that profits have to be shared out among a large number of people, meaning that the original founders of the enterprise may lose control as more people buy shares. [4 marks]

(d) A franchise could be a useful type of business organisation for a new enterprise, as a franchise arrangement has a number of potential advantages. The franchisee is able to sell a recognised branded product and so the revenue received from the sales of the enterprise is likely to be quite large. Some of the advertising will be carried out by the franchisor, keeping down the costs of advertising by the franchisee, a potentially important fact for a new enterprise just starting up. Also, a franchise arrangement is likely to be less risky than starting up an enterprise with a new name because the branded product will be familiar to many people, so there is likely to be less risk of failure. Finally, certain services, such as training, may be carried out by the franchisor, saving the franchisee money. For all of these reasons, a franchise arrangement could be a good choice of business organisation for a new enterprise. [8 marks]

Total: 17 out of 29

Examiner feedback

a. The candidate has defined the term 'action plan' in terms of a plan that outlines the actions required to achieve particular aims and objectives, but has not gone on to state that an action plan provides a way of monitoring the progress of an enterprise.

b. The explanation of why it is important for an enterprise to monitor the progress of its action plan is a good effort and gained all four marks.

c. Unfortunately, the candidate only described one advantage and one disadvantage of a limited company as a business organisation for a new enterprise, and so only four of the maximum eight marks could be given.

The candidate needed to describe one other potential advantage, such as the fact that the shareholders in an enterprise have limited liability which means that they cannot lose their personal possessions if the enterprise gets into difficulty and goes bankrupt.

The candidate also needed to describe one other potential disadvantage, such as the fact that there is often a divorce or separation of ownership and control, unlike the situation with a sole trader or a partnership, which combine ownership and control.

d. The candidate has considered a number of the potential advantages of a franchise arrangement for a new enterprise, but the answer is entirely one-sided with no consideration of the possible disadvantages.

For example, the franchisee would need to make a payment to the franchisor for the franchise rights and this payment would usually still have to be made even if a loss was made by the franchisee. In addition to this payment, the franchisee would normally be required to pay a percentage of the income received from sales to the franchisor each year. The franchisor may strictly control the activities of the franchisee, giving it little choice in many aspects of business, and this can therefore be regarded as very restrictive by the franchisee.

The candidate, having considered both the advantages and the disadvantages of a franchise arrangement, could have then come to a conclusion as to whether a franchise would have been the best type of business organisation for a new enterprise.

Unit 3:
Enterprise skills

Your exam

Enterprise skills is part of Component 1: Written Paper, and Component 2: Coursework.

Component 1 is a 90-minute exam and makes up 50% of the total marks.
Component 2 is the coursework and makes up 50% of the total marks.

Your revision checklist

Tick these boxes to build a record of your revision

Specification	Theme	Tick
3.1 Skills of enterprising people	Skills required by entrepreneurs	
	Identifying and evaluating your own enterprise skills	
3.2 Behaviours of entrepreneurs	How entrepreneurs use their enterprise skills	

You need to know:
- the skills that enterprising people should have
- how to identify and evaluate your own skills during your enterprise project.

Skills required by entrepreneurs

The practical skills and knowledge to create products

Entrepreneurs need to possess the necessary practical and technical skills to put their ideas into effect. A good example of such an entrepreneur is Sir James Dyson, the inventor of the bagless vacuum cleaner.

Leadership

The quality of leadership will be crucial to the success of an enterprise.

- Leadership is concerned with qualities such as decisiveness and the ability to think ahead, especially in relation to seeing opportunities, anticipating problems and sensing and responding to change.

- Effective leadership is based on the ability to exercise good judgment, to take the correct decisions and to make others want to share the leader's vision and mission.

- If a leader has a charismatic, imaginative, energetic, ambitious, courageous and inspirational personality it helps people to believe in that leader.

There are three distinct leadership styles:

- *autocratic*: a leader takes all the major decisions
- *democratic*: others are encouraged to be involved in decision-making
- *laissez-faire*: employees have relatively few guidelines or directions.

> **Exam tip**
>
> You should understand the difference between leadership and management. Sir Alex Ferguson, the manager of Manchester United between 1986 and 2013, stated: "My job was to make everyone understand that the impossible was possible. That's the difference between leadership and management."

Influencing skills

- A successful entrepreneur should be able to influence others using good interpersonal and communication skills.

- This will apply to the range of stakeholders that have an interest in an enterprise.

Team-building

- It is important to be able to build an effective team to offer support.

- It will be difficult for an entrepreneur to succeed without a strong team around them.

> **Exam tip**
>
> You need to understand that the term 'skills' can be used to cover attributes, characteristics and learned skills.

> **Exam tip**
>
> You need to understand that different people combine and use enterprise skills in many ways.

 **Key terms**

> **Leadership style:** the distinctive way in which decisions are taken in an enterprise
>
> **Team-building:** the process of improving the effectiveness and motivation of people working together in a team

⊗ **Common error**

> Candidates sometimes confuse a democratic and a laissez-faire style of leadership, but they are distinct styles.

⊗ **Common error**

> Leadership and management are sometimes confused, but it is important to distinguish between them.

Key terms

Delegation: where responsibility is passed down to others in an enterprise

Innovation: the process of putting a new idea into practice

Delegation

- Entrepreneurs cannot make every decision so they need to delegate to others.
- Choosing the right people to complete a particular job or task effectively is an important entrepreneurial skill.

Problem-solving

- Entrepreneurs need to have the vision and commitment to look at a problem from different perspectives – 'thinking outside the box'.
- The solutions may be seen as radical or innovative.

Prioritisation and time management

- Entrepreneurs need to prioritise jobs; decide which are more important than others.
- If entrepreneurs allow themselves to be 'sidetracked' on less important tasks it could affect the success of an enterprise.
- Successful entrepreneurs also needs to be able to organise their time efficiently.
- Effective time management is absolutely crucial to the success of an entrepreneur.

Exam tip

You need to recognise that some people have these enterprise skills naturally and that others have to develop them, such as self-confidence.

Self-confidence

- The leaders of enterprises should have confidence in their product and in their ability to succeed.
- A positive self-image will reflect positively on the reputation of the enterprise.

Exam tip

You need to show that you understand the possible link between self-confidence and the potential success of an enterprise.

Resourcefulness

- Entrepreneurs need to be resourceful.
- This means that they need to have, or be able to gain, the resources required to achieve the success of an enterprise.

Innovation

- Innovation refers to the process of putting a new idea into practice.
- There are two types of innovation:
  - product innovation, where a new product is brought into the marketplace
  - process innovation, where new ways of doing something are introduced.
- Entrepreneurs are often innovative by coming up with new ideas and developing new products.
- They often challenge traditional and orthodox approaches and look at new ways to solve problems.
- Steve Jobs, the founder of Apple, stated that it is innovation, more than anything else, that distinguishes a leader from a follower.

Exam tip

Make sure you can demonstrate that you clearly understand the difference between an invention, which refers to a totally original idea, and an innovation, which refers to putting a new idea into practice.

Taking initiative

- The willingness to take the initiative is likely to be crucial to the success of an enterprise.
- This means that an entrepreneur should not wait to see what happens, but should be bold and decisive in making a decision.
- This is where the judgment of an entrepreneur is crucial.

Taking calculated risks

- Customers decide the success or failure of an enterprise project.
- Only one in five new products is successful – so an 80% risk of failure.
- Despite this, entrepreneurs continue to take the calculated risk of introducing new products.
- If an enterprise project does fail, then the entrepreneur should learn from mistakes made.

Taking responsibility

- Being able to make decisions and take responsibility, especially in difficult times, is absolutely crucial to the success of an entrepreneur.

Motivation and a determination to succeed

- An entrepreneur needs to be well-motivated and determined to succeed.
- Many enterprises collapse, especially during the first year, so the entrepreneur must be fully committed to the project in order to succeed.

Creativity

- Entrepreneurs need to be able to put their creative and original ideas into practice.
- They need to be bold because of the fear of failure.
- Edwin Land, the inventor of the Polaroid camera, once said that "an essential aspect of creativity is not being afraid to fail".

Perseverance

- An entrepreneur needs to persevere, especially when the enterprise project is experiencing difficulties.
- This is why a vision with a goal to work towards is so important.

Identifying and evaluating your own enterprise skills

In Task 3 of the coursework project, you must identify five of your own enterprise skills used during the project and how you used these skills, one of which must be negotiation. You will need to submit a written record of how you used these five skills to implement your enterprise project. You must only write about your own enterprise skills.

You will also need to evaluate these skills. It will be helpful if you keep a skills audit in which you can rate your enterprise skills, i.e. from strong to weak.

 Key term

Perseverance: the determination and persistence to achieve something despite experiencing difficulties

 Coursework tip

You will be given the opportunity to identify and evaluate your own enterprise skills during the enterprise project. It will be helpful if you keep a record of the skills you have used throughout your enterprise project.

You need to know:

- some named entrepreneurs from the local community, wider society or even in your own school
- how the entrepreneurs studied used enterprise skills.

How entrepreneurs use their enterprise skills

You should be familiar with entrepreneurs from the local community and from the wider society in the rest of the world. You should be able to recognise how particular entrepreneurs have used their enterprise skills.

 Recap

- Enterprise skills may include:
    - the practical skills and knowledge to create products
    - leadership
    - influencing skills
    - team-building
    - delegation
    - problem-solving
    - prioritisation and time management
    - self-confidence
    - resourcefulness
    - innovation
    - taking initiative
    - taking calculated risks
    - taking responsibility
    - motivation and a determination to succeed
    - creativity
    - perseverance.

- You will need to identify and evaluate five of your own skills during your enterprise project.

 Review

Entrepreneurs use their wide range of skills in a variety of ways to help make their enterprise a success. No two entrepreneurs and no two enterprises are the same, and so it is important that you fully appreciate the importance of the various enterprise skills.

Case studies are particularly helpful in stressing the link between enterprise skills and the success of an entrepreneur. There are a number of these in the Student Book to help you understand this link:

Sir James Dyson (page 40)   Jennifer Liu (page 45)

Ambareesh Murty (page 41)   Frans Aupa Indongo (page 45)

Sir Richard Branson (page 42)   Gossy Ukanwoke (page 46)

Shimi Shah (page 43)   Tendai Theresa Mashanda (page 46)

Steve Jobs (page 44)   Madinah Nalukenge (page 47)

Nkemdilim Begho (page 44)   Attoysius Attah (page 48)

Anya Cherneff (page 44)   Hooi Ling Tan (page 49).

Apply

1. Explain why leadership and team-building are two important enterprise skills.

2. Analyse how one entrepreneur you have studied has used enterprise skills to be successful.

Analysis

✓ In (a), you will need to clearly define what is meant by the term 'innovation'.

✓ In (b), you will need to focus on providing an explanation of why time management is an important enterprise skill.

✓ In (c), you will need to give a clear analysis of why self-confidence is important if an entrepreneur is to be successful.

✓ In (d), you will need to provide a clear discussion of whether motivation and a determination to succeed are likely to be crucial to the success of an entrepreneur.

Mark scheme

a. One mark for stating that innovation refers to the process of putting a new idea into practice; one mark for stating that there are actually two types of innovation: product innovation, where a new product is brought into the marketplace, and process innovation, where new ways of doing something are introduced.

b. Up to four marks for an explanation of why time management is an important enterprise skill, pointing out that entrepreneurs need to concentrate on the important aspects of their work, which will involve deciding what is more important than something else – prioritising jobs. Successful entrepreneurs also need to organise themselves as efficiently as possible. A key element of this is the organisation of time; effective time management is absolutely crucial to the success of an entrepreneur.

c. Up to six marks for an analysis of why self-confidence is important if an entrepreneur is to be successful, stressing that it is important that entrepreneurs are confident in themselves, especially in their ability to succeed, and in their product and their enterprise. Confident entrepreneurs are those who are convinced that their enterprise idea will be a success and self-confidence will help a person to have a positive self-image, which reflects positively on the reputation of the enterprise.

d. Knowledge and understanding, Level 1, 1–3 marks; some analysis, Level 2, 4–7 marks; good analysis, Level 3, 8–10 marks.

Raise your grade

Student answer

(a) Innovation is the process of putting a new idea into practice. [1 mark]

(b) Time management is an important enterprise skill because organisation is crucial to the success of an enterprise and this includes the organisation of time. Effective time management is absolutely crucial to the success of an enterprise. [2 marks]

(c) Self-confidence is important if an entrepreneur is to be successful because others need to see that the entrepreneur has confidence in his or her own ability, in the good or service that is being sold, and in the enterprise generally. This will help to enhance the level of motivation and commitment of all the stakeholders connected with an enterprise. [3 marks]

(d) Motivation and a determination to succeed will be important in the success of an entrepreneur. Many enterprises collapse during the first year of operation, so it is important that the entrepreneur remains committed to, and passionate about, what the enterprise stands for. It is important that he or she has a clear vision for the enterprise and stays focused on this vision and on what needs to be done in order to achieve it. [4 marks]

Total: 10 out of 22

 Examiner feedback

a. The candidate has defined the term 'innovation' as the process of putting a new idea into practice. To gain the second mark there needed to be a reference to the fact that there are actually two types of innovation: product innovation, where a new product is brought into the marketplace, and process innovation, where new ways of doing something are introduced. The candidate could also have distinguished between an innovation and an invention.

b. The candidate has made some attempt to explain why time management is an important enterprise skill, but the explanation could have been developed more fully. For example, the candidate could have pointed out that entrepreneurs need to concentrate on the important and significant aspects of their work and that this will involve them in deciding what is more important than something else, i.e. an entrepreneur needs to prioritise jobs that are more important than others.

c. The candidate has made a reasonable attempt to analyse why self-confidence is important if an entrepreneur is to be successful, but additional marks would have been gained if there had been reference to the demonstration of an entrepreneur's confidence in his or her ability to succeed and to the idea of a positive self-image reflecting positively on the reputation of the enterprise.

d. The candidate had made some attempt to consider whether motivation and a determination to succeed are likely to be crucial to the success of an entrepreneur, pointing out the importance of being committed and passionate. There are also useful comments on the potential significance of vision, but the candidate could have gone on to consider some of the other skills that help to make an enterprise a success, such as resourcefulness, the ability and willingness to take calculated risks and the demonstration of both creativity and perseverance.

Unit 4:
Enterprise opportunities, risk, legal obligations and ethical considerations

Your exam

Enterprise opportunities, risk, legal obligations and ethical considerations are part of Component 1: Written Paper, and Component 2: Coursework.

Component 1 is a 90-minute exam and makes up 50% of the total marks.
Component 2 is the coursework and makes up 50% of the total marks.

Your revision checklist

Tick these boxes to build a record of your revision

Specification	Theme	Tick
4.1 Enterprise opportunities	How enterprise opportunities arise	
4.2 Risk	Risks involved in an enterprise	
	Identifying risks: SWOT analysis	
	Identifying risks: PEST analysis	
	Analysing and managing risks	
	Attitudes to risk	
4.3 Legal obligations	Laws and regulations and their impact	
4.4 Ethical considerations	The impact of an enterprise on communities and society	
	Ethical considerations within an enterprise	
	The impact of ethical considerations on the operation of an enterprise	

You need to know:

- how enterprise opportunities arise through
  o changing needs or wants for a product
  o change in the ability to meet needs or wants
  o advances in technology
  o changes in government policy.

How enterprise opportunities arise

It is possible to identify four possible reasons that demonstrate how enterprise opportunities arise.

Exam tip

It is important to recognise that opportunities for enterprise may be local, national, international or global.

Exam tip

Make sure you understand the difference between income and real income. An increase in real income refers to an increase in income that is above the rate of inflation in a particular country. For example, if inflation in a country is 2% per annum and incomes have risen by 5% for the year, then the increase in real income is the difference, i.e. 3%.

 Key term

Real income: the increase in income after subtracting the rate of inflation

Opportunity	Explanation
Changing needs or wants for a product	• Changes in tastes and fashion affect demand for products. Entrepreneurs need to understand that, over time, some products will become less popular while others will become more popular. They need to anticipate those products for which demand may increase in the future.
	• Changes in the size and structure of population can influence demand for products. An increase in population means there will be more potential customers, making the success of an enterprise more likely. Changes in the age distribution may affect the potential demand for particular products. For example, in many countries there is an ageing population. If an enterprise focused on products for this age group, the increase in the number of such people would be likely to enhance its chance of success.
	• Demand for products is influenced by changes in real income (changes in income related to the rate of inflation).
Change in the ability to meet needs or wants	• Opportunities for enterprise arise not only from demand but also from supply.
	• Changes in the ability to meet needs or wants can come about as the result of new production methods that enterprises are able to use.
Advances in technology	• New products, such as smart phones, widen consumer choice and are the result of the application of new technology and of research and development. Such development provides enormous opportunities for enterprise initiatives.
Changes in government policy	• Governments can provide financial support for enterprises, such as through grants and subsidies, and/or support through information and advice.
	• Governments can make favourable changes in taxation, such as charging a lower rate of taxation (even zero) to enterprises in the early stages of development.
	• Governments can make favourable changes in the law, such as by making it easier for enterprises to start up in certain areas of a country.

Recap

Enterprise opportunities can arise from:

- changing needs or wants for a product
- changes in the ability to meet needs or wants
- advances in technology
- changes in government policy.

 Apply

Explain how changes in both the size and the structure of population can give rise to enterprise opportunities.

 Review

It is important that you are able to identify possible reasons for how enterprise opportunities can arise. These can be local, national, international or global reasons, such as changing needs or wants for a product, changes in the ability of enterprises to meet those needs or wants, advances in technology and changes in government policy.

The Student Book includes four case studies to aid your understanding of enterprise opportunities:

Hotel du Vin, in relation to changes in the tastes of consumers (page 52)

MarketInvoice, in relation to the development of the internet (page 54)

Bookmyforex.com, in relation to changes in real incomes (page 53)

eBay, in relation to the opportunities presented by globalisation (page 55).

Exam tip

You need to appreciate that enterprise opportunities can arise from both the demand side and the supply side; and also from changes in the size and structure of the population.

Exam tip

Opportunities for enterprise may be local, national, international or global. Globalisation is an important development that has given entrepreneurs the opportunity to create an enterprise, and sell in more than one country.

 **Key term**

Globalisation: the trend towards worldwide markets in goods and services

You need to know:

- that there are financial, economic, health and safety or environmental, human resources and production risks
- about the identification of risks (SWOT and PEST)
- how to analyse and manage risks
- entrepreneurs' attitudes to risk (risk-averse, risk-reducer, risk-keen).

 Key terms

Unique selling point (USP): a feature of a product that makes it different from other similar products, and therefore more attractive to people who might buy it

Working capital: the finance required by an enterprise to pay for the costs of production until payment is received for the output that has been produced

Exam tip

Make sure you understand that risk is an inevitable feature of enterprise.

Risks involved in an enterprise

Risk	Explanation
Financial	• An enterprise may not be able to secure the finance that it needs. This is often in relation to working capital. There may be funding to establish an enterprise, but then not enough money to pay everyday costs, such as wages. • Perhaps the biggest risk to an enterprise comes from cash flow problems. Examples of financial risks can include an unexpected increase in costs and lower than expected sales.
Economic	• Economic risks can include changes in the economic environment. For example, high levels of unemployment can make it more difficult for an enterprise to sell its products. • Market research is important for an enterprise to find out what the customers want. There is always the risk that the market research has not produced accurate and reliable data. • The enterprise needs to attract customers through a distinctive unique selling point (USP), and then retain them. The risk is that customers will not recognise the USP as sufficiently distinctive. • There is a risk that an identified gap in the market will not be large enough for the enterprise to be profitable.
Health and safety or environmental	• Enterprises have legal responsibilities to both employees and customers, especially in relation to health and safety laws and regulations. • Enterprises must comply with environmental laws and regulations. Failure to do so could lead to an enterprise being fined or even closed down.
Human resources	• An enterprise runs the risk that employees may not have the necessary skills, qualifications, experience or expertise.
Production	• An enterprise needs to deliver on its promises. • An enterprise will need to ensure that its production and distribution resources are sufficient for supply to meet demand.

Identifying risks: SWOT analysis

SWOT feature	Explanation
Strengths	The internal characteristics of an enterprise that give it an advantage over others, e.g. • abundant and good quality resources • management and leadership • the competitive advantage over rivals, such as lower costs and superior products • a loyal and productive workforce and a good product range.
Weaknesses	The internal characteristics of an enterprise that place it at a disadvantage to others, e.g. • limitations in production, such as a large amount of spare manufacturing capacity • ineffective marketing • a poorly trained workforce • ageing capital equipment.
Opportunities	Elements in the external environment that an enterprise could exploit to its advantage, e.g. • immediate opportunities in its present markets, or the long-term strategic possibilities of expanding markets, such as export markets • diversification into new markets, which would include the potential areas of expansion of the enterprise and future profits • lower rates of interest leading to increase in consumer demand; and the application of new technologies, both in terms of products and methods of production.
Threats	Elements in the external environment that could cause difficulties for an enterprise. Threats could include: • losing out to existing competitors and to new entrants into a market • an adverse change in market conditions • globalisation forcing down prices • changes in the law and changes in government policy.

 Key term

SWOT analysis: an acronym for *strengths*, *weaknesses*, *opportunities* and *threats*; it is a structured planning method that evaluates these four elements of an enterprise

 Common error

Candidates sometimes fail to clearly distinguish between the internal and external elements of a SWOT analysis. In a SWOT analysis, the strengths and weaknesses refer to internal elements within an enterprise whereas the opportunities and threats refer to external elements.

Key terms

PEST analysis: the analysis of the wider macro-environment of an enterprise, including *political, economic, social* and *technological* factors

Product life cycle: the typical sales pattern of a product over time from its introduction in a market to its eventual decline

Technology: the use of tools, machines and science in the production of goods

Exam tip

Make sure you can think of new products and also new ways of working when you are considering the potential impact of technological change on enterprises.

Exam tip

Make sure you understand the four factors that are included in a PEST analysis.

▲ **Figure 1** *A political factor: voting in Uganda*

Identifying risks: PEST analysis

PEST factor	Explanation
Political	Activities of enterprises can be affected by political decisions, e.g. • An increase in the rate of taxation will mean that enterprises may have to pay higher taxes on their profits. Disposable incomes of people will be reduced, negatively impacting on the products provided by an enterprise. • A government may offer financial support through grants and subsidies. A new government may stop this support.
Economic	Decisions are taken that affect the wider (or macro) economy, but these decisions will also have an impact on particular enterprises at a microeconomic level, e.g. • An economy facing a high inflation rate may increase interest rates to try to bring inflation down. This would make it more expensive for an enterprise and for potential customers to borrow money, so borrowing to finance spending would be less likely. • Lowering the exchange rate (depreciation or devaluation) may encourage the purchase of exports in other countries, which would be advantageous to an enterprise that exports a large number of products. But there is a risk that imports will be more expensive. This would be a disadvantage to an enterprise that imports a lot of its raw materials and component parts.
Social	Enterprises can be affected by social factors, such as changes in the size and structure of a region's or a country's population: • Religious groups may be a factor in having a social impact on an enterprise, e.g. certain groups may not be inclined to buy particular products, affecting the sales of an enterprise. This is a risk faced by enterprises if such a group becomes more influential. • The migration of people, both from one country to another, and from one part of a country to another, can have a social impact on enterprises, e.g. in many countries, there has been migration from rural areas to urban areas. This could negatively affect enterprises in one part of a country, and positively affect enterprises in other parts of a country.
Technological	Technology and, in particular, the level of technology can provide opportunities for enterprises, e.g. • Advances in technical knowledge are opening up new product markets and new ways of producing goods. Technological progress also offers potential risks, e.g. • The speed of technological change may mean that some goods will have a shorter life cycle than was previously the case. • Developments in technology may mean there is a move away from more traditional methods of working. There is a risk that this could lead to lower levels of motivation among the workforce of an enterprise.

▲ **Figure 2** *An economic factor: stacked containers on an ocean freighter*

▲ **Figure 3** *A social factor: a crowded urban development in Mexico City*

▲ **Figure 4** *A technological factor: the use of robots in car production in the Czech Republic*

Analysing and managing risks

Identifying risks and analysing the implications of each risk

- Both SWOT analysis and PEST analysis are extremely useful in identifying the risks faced by an enterprise. However, an important feature of the enterprise process is balancing the potential negative outcomes against the potential positive outcomes, i.e. balancing the risks against the rewards.

- A financial objective, to make money and become richer, is clearly important. Although maximising profit is the main goal of many enterprises, many enterprises are not-for-profit organisations that have social, rather than monetary, objectives. Such organisations are becoming increasingly important in many countries.

- Another reason for people starting an enterprise is because they want to be in control, i.e. they want to be their own boss and take the important decisions themselves. Their main goal, therefore, is to gain a sense of achievement when an enterprise becomes a success.

Deciding if the risk is worth taking

- The result of balancing the potential negative outcomes against the potential positive outcomes is to decide whether the risk is worth taking.

- An entrepreneur may decide to go ahead with an enterprise project, despite the risks, in the hope that the rewards of the project will make such a decision worthwhile.

- After due consideration of the potential risks, an entrepreneur may decide to reject an enterprise idea.

Planning how to manage the risks

Once an entrepreneur has taken the decision to go ahead with an enterprise idea, he or she must plan how to manage the risks involved:

- It is important to identify those risks that can be dealt with and are worth dealing with. This will involve the enterprise determining a response strategy.

- An enterprise will tend to focus on those risks over which it has some form of control, e.g. ensuring that the capital needs of the enterprise are sufficient and that there are enough employees with the necessary skills and experience.

Once an enterprise has determined a response strategy to deal with particular risks, it will need to monitor progress in dealing with those risks, to see if it is necessary to amend the response strategy. A management plan is likely to focus on avoiding the risk but, if this is not possible, it will aim to minimise the risk by taking appropriate actions.

There are also likely to be certain situations, especially where the aim of an enterprise is to maximise profits, where the plan focuses on maximising the risk.

Exam tip

Risk can be approached in terms of a four-stage process:

- identify risks

- analyse the implications of each risk

- decide if the risk is worth taking or not

- plan how to manage the risks.

Attitudes to risk

The ways in which a particular entrepreneur deals with risk will depend on whether the person is *risk-averse*, a *risk reducer* or *risk-keen*.

Risk-averse

An entrepreneur who is risk-averse avoids taking risks. Risk avoidance is a risk management technique that aims to eliminate any possibility of risk.

Risk reducer

A risk reducer has a relatively low tolerance of risk and will aim to reduce the level of risk and uncertainty to a level that is acceptable to an enterprise. The potential risk of failure will be reduced but so also will the potential reward or profit for the enterprise. This approach to risk management may be more likely when there is uncertainty, such as during an economic recession.

Risk-keen

This attitude to risk tends to apply to those entrepreneurs who aim to maximise profits. It is often the case that where there is a high expectation of profit, there will also be a high level of risk.

 Recap

1. Risks involved in enterprise may be in the following areas:
   - financial
   - economic
   - human resources
   - health and safety or environmental
   - production.

2. Risks can be identified through a SWOT (strengths, weaknesses, opportunities and threats) analysis and a PEST (political, economic, social and technological) analysis.

3. Entrepreneurs need to analyse the implications of each risk by balancing the potential negative outcomes against the potential positive outcomes.

4. Entrepreneurs need to decide if the risk is worth taking and may come to the conclusion that some risks would lead to the rejection of an enterprise idea.

5. Entrepreneurs need to plan how to manage the risks by avoiding, minimising or maximising the risk.

6. An entrepreneur can be risk-averse, a risk reducer or risk-keen. Different attitudes to risk can affect how an entrepreneur manages the risk.

Apply

1. Explain how economic factors could create a risk for an enterprise.

2. Explain the key features of a SWOT analysis of an enterprise.

Review

Make sure you are aware of different ways of identifying, analysing and managing risks and of different attitudes to risk. Case studies can help you to understand that an element of risk is an inevitable feature of enterprise.

There are two case studies in the Student Book that focus on risk: Tom Ravenscroft, the founder of Enabling Enterprise, in relation to the human resource risks of enterprise (page 58), and Ashish Dhawan, the founder of ChrysCapital, in relation to the recognition of the inevitability of risk in enterprise (page 68).

You need to know:
- why laws and regulations are needed to protect stakeholders
- the impact of laws and regulations on all stakeholders in these areas.

Laws and regulations and their impact

Area	Explanation
Employment	• Laws can apply to the recruitment of employees, their contracts and redundancy. There is a risk to an enterprise of dismissing a worker incorrectly, leading to possible court action. • Laws can also relate to health and safety at work and an enterprise needs to ensure that it provides an appropriate working environment. If this does not happen, an enterprise risks being taken to court if an employee is injured at work. • In some countries, there is a legal minimum wage. An enterprise must ensure that it complies with such legislation, otherwise it risks being accused of operating illegally. • An enterprise must respect the legal rights and responsibilities of trade unions, otherwise it could be taken to court.
Production	• The law can also apply to production. Health and safety laws, in particular, affect the production process of an enterprise, e.g. protective clothing and certain equipment may need to be provided by an enterprise. This can increase the costs for an enterprise, but it risks being taken to court by an employee if such laws are not respected.
Marketing and selling	• In some countries there are laws restricting marketing activities, such as what an enterprise can say in an advertisement. This can pose a risk to an enterprise as false claims about a product can lead to legal action. • Pressure groups can try to influence the advertising of particular products. For example, in the UK, Action on Smoking and Health (ASH) campaigns against the advertising of cigarettes. • In many countries, there are laws that aim to protect the consumer in different ways, restricting the freedom of an enterprise and what it sells, such as: ◦ the products or services should be fit to sell, e.g. they should be safe ◦ they should be suitable for the purpose indicated ◦ they should perform and operate in the way described. There will be a risk to an enterprise of being taken to court if it makes claims about a product it is selling that are untrue.
Finance	• Laws and regulations can affect how enterprises organise their finances, how they report on them, the roles and responsibilities of directors, the payment of taxes and how their financial statements are presented.

 Recap

Laws and regulations to protect stakeholders are needed in the areas of:
- employment
- production
- marketing and selling
- finance.

 Apply

Explain why laws and regulations to protect stakeholders are needed in the area of marketing and selling.

 **Review**

Laws and regulations are important in influencing how enterprises operate, especially in relation to their various stakeholders, because they establish what enterprises must do, what they should do, what they can do and what they must not do. You will not be required to know the details of specific laws and regulations.

Exam tip

You will not be assessed on specific laws, but you could be assessed on the impact of laws and regulations on stakeholders in the above four areas.

You need to know:

- that the impact of an enterprise on communities and society may be positive or negative
- that enterprises, such as Fairtrade, can be run following moral values and beliefs
- how ethical considerations can impact on the operation of an enterprise.

Key terms

Corporate social responsibility: the willingness of an enterprise to accept responsibility for its actions and how they may impact on a variety of stakeholders

Pressure group: an organisation that aims to influence governments and enterprises to adopt policies and actions it favours

Social impact of enterprise: the impact, either positive or negative, that an enterprise may have on communities and society

▲ **Figure 5** *A member of the Greenpeace pressure group monitoring the outflow into a river*

▲ **Figure 6** *Organic cotton farming in India*

The impact of an enterprise on communities and society

It is important to have an awareness of how an enterprise may have a positive or a negative impact on communities and society:

- *Positive impact*: many enterprises support local communities through activities such as sporting events and amateur dramatic productions. This positive approach to social and community issues is part of what is generally known as 'corporate social responsibility'.

- *Negative impact*: some enterprises contribute to traffic congestion, noise pollution, air pollution, water pollution, the use of non-renewable natural resources and emissions of gases that can possibly lead to the process of global warming.

Ethical considerations within an enterprise

Ethical considerations can apply within enterprises that aim to behave in a socially responsible way by applying ethical and moral principles to what they do and how they do it. Examples of such enterprises include:

- Fairtrade

- enterprises dedicated to organic farming, where traditional farming methods are employed that use environmentally sound techniques free from synthetic pesticides, growth hormones and antibiotics

- enterprises that donate a proportion of their profits to charities.

Fairtrade

Fairtrade products carry the Fairtrade Mark, which signifies that:

- the producers have received a fair price for their produce

- the price covers the cost of sustainable production

- there is a long-term relationship with buyers, helping producers plan for the future

- the producers receive an extra sum of money, called the Fairtrade Premium, which can be spent in local communities, such as improved sanitation, health centres or educational facilities

- producers are accountable for their use of the Fairtrade Premium.

As well as the above, their workers:

- must be paid a fair wage

- must have decent working conditions

- are guaranteed the right to join trade unions

- are provided with good housing, where relevant.

In many countries, there are groups who support the ethical and moral principles of Fairtrade. For example, all such groups in the county of Oxfordshire, UK are joined together through 'Fairtrade in Oxfordshire'.

The impact of ethical considerations on the operation of an enterprise

Ethical and moral principles can apply to all aspects of an enterprise, including:

- who it buys its supplies from
- how it treats its employees
- how it acts towards its competitors
- what impact it has on the environment
- what impact it has on the local community.

▲ **Figure 7** *The Fairtrade Mark; by choosing to buy Fairtrade products, you can be sure you are making a difference*

 Recap

You need to know:

- how an enterprise may have positive and negative impacts on communities and society
- how an enterprise can demonstrate ethical considerations, e.g. by being run on moral values and beliefs, such as Fairtrade
- how ethical considerations can impact on the operation of an enterprise.

 Key term

Ethical principle: a way of doing something according to a set of moral principles, values and beliefs

Exam tip

Make sure you know what is distinctive about Fairtrade products. They guarantee that producers in the developing world are getting a fairer deal.

 Apply

Describe the main features of Fairtrade.

Review

Ethics and ethical considerations can have a key influence on an enterprise. Many enterprises operate according to a set of moral principles, values and beliefs, and these principles can often form part of the vision or mission of an enterprise, helping to define what it is and what it represents. An example of such an enterprise is Fairtrade.

On pages 74–75 of the Student Book, there is a case study on Agrocel, a Fairtrade Organic Cotton Project in India that is based on the idea of a fair wage for its workers and on the recognition of the importance of sustainability.

Exam tip

You need to know how an enterprise can demonstrate ethical and moral principles in carrying out its work.

Sample question

1. **a.** Define the term 'real income'. [2]

    b. Explain what is meant when one entrepreneur is described as being 'risk-averse' and another is described as being 'risk-keen'. [4]

    c. Explain the political factors that could play a part in a PEST analysis of an enterprise. [6]

    d. Analyse the potential impact of ethical considerations within an enterprise and on the operation of an enterprise. [10]

Analysis

✓ In (a), you will need to clearly define what is meant by the term 'real income'.

✓ In (b), you will need to focus on providing an explanation of what is meant when one entrepreneur is described as being 'risk-averse' and another is described as 'risk-keen'.

✓ In (c), you will need to explain the political factors that could play a part in a PEST analysis of an enterprise.

✓ In (d), you will need to analyse, and not just describe, the potential impact of ethical considerations within an enterprise and on the operation of an enterprise.

Mark scheme

a. One mark for stating that real income is an income level that has been adjusted to take into account the effect of inflation; one mark for stating that it is calculated by subtracting the rate of inflation from the increase in income.

b. Up to two marks for an explanation of what is meant when one entrepreneur is described as being 'risk-averse'; up to two marks for an explanation of what is meant when one entrepreneur is described as being 'risk-keen'.

c. Up to six marks for an explanation of the political factors that could play a part in a PEST analysis of an enterprise.

d. Knowledge and understanding, Level 1, 1–3 marks; some analysis, Level 2, 4–7 marks; good analysis, Level 3, 8–10 marks.

Student answer

(a) An increase in real income refers to an increase in income that is above the rate of inflation. Real income refers to an income that has been adjusted to take into account the effect of inflation. It is calculated by subtracting the rate of inflation from the increase in income. [2 marks]

(b) When an entrepreneur is described as risk-averse, it means an attitude to risk characterised by being unwilling to take any risk. When an entrepreneur is described as risk-keen, it means an attitude to risk which recognises that a high level of risk may have advantages for an enterprise. [2 marks]

(c) There are a number of political factors that could play a part in a PEST analysis of an enterprise. A government could decide to increase the rate of taxation. This means that enterprises may have to pay higher taxes on their profits, leaving them with less money to reinvest into the enterprises. It also means that if taxes on income are increased, the disposable incomes of people, i.e. their spending power, will be reduced and this could have a negative impact on the products provided by an enterprise. [3 marks]

(d) Ethical considerations can have an important impact on enterprises, both within an enterprise and on the operation of an enterprise. Ethical considerations can apply within an enterprise, such as when an enterprise is organised and run on the basis of a number of moral values and beliefs and ethical principles. Such enterprises have as one of their objectives the need to behave in a socially responsible and accountable way by applying ethical and moral values and principles to what they do and how they do it. Such enterprises are committed to the principle of corporate social responsibility, i.e. the willingness of an enterprise to accept responsibility for its actions and how they may impact on a variety of stakeholders. Examples of such enterprises include Fairtrade, enterprises dedicated to organic farming and enterprises that are willing to donate some of their profits to particular charities. [5 marks]

Total: 12 out of 22

✓ Examiner feedback

a. The candidate has given a good definition of real income and how it is calculated, gaining both marks.

b. The candidate has given the meanings of the two terms, but the explanations really needed to be developed more fully in order to gain further marks. For example, in relation to risk-averse, the candidate could have expanded on the point about being unwilling to take any risk by explaining that an entrepreneur with such an attitude to risk will be much less likely to see an enterprise collapse. In relation to an entrepreneur being risk-keen, the candidate could have expanded on some of the possible advantages for an enterprise, such as a high level of profit.

c. The candidate has referred to some political factors, mainly in connection with taxation, and there was scope to have developed the answer more fully. For example, the candidate could have referred to the possibility that it may have been the policy of one government to support enterprises by giving them different forms of grant or subsidy to help them financially. If an election was to take place, and the government is replaced by another, there will be no guarantee that the policies of the previous government will be continued. It could be that the new government decides to try to save money by discontinuing the financial help, making it more difficult for enterprises to survive.

d. The candidate has made quite a good attempt to analyse the potential impact of ethical considerations within an enterprise, but has not gone on to consider the possible impact on the operation of an enterprise. For example, the candidate could have analysed how ethical and moral principles could apply to the operation of an enterprise, such as who it buys its supplies from, how it treats its employees, how it acts towards its competitors and what impact it has on the environment and on the local community.

Unit 5:
Negotiation

Your exam

Negotiation is part of Component 1: Written Paper, and Component 2: Coursework.

Component 1 is a 90-minute exam and makes up 50% of the total marks.
Component 2 is the coursework and makes up 50% of the total marks.

Your revision checklist

Tick these boxes to build a record of your revision

Specification	Theme	Tick
5.1 The negotiation process	The process of negotiation	
	Stages in the negotiation process	

You need to know:
- what negotiation is
- the stages in the negotiation process – planning, conducting and measuring the success of the negotiation.

The process of negotiation

Part of process	Explanation
Resolving disputes	• Negotiation involves two or more people or parties coming together in an attempt to reach an understanding. • Negotiation can range from informal processes, as with family and friends, to more formal processes, as with an enterprise. • With formal negotiation, an agenda outlines what is to be discussed. The order of times on the agenda may actually influence the outcome of the negotiation.
Agreeing upon courses of action	The different parties will adopt courses of action, or tactics, that they think will bring about a successful outcome. Two kinds of negotiating strategy can be recognised: • *Distributive* negotiation is based on a hard-bargaining position – if one negotiator wins, the other must lose. It can therefore be viewed as a 'win-lose' situation. • *Integrative* negotiation is based on reaching an agreement recognising the interests of all those involved in the process – a 'win-win' situation.
Bargaining for individual or collective advantage	• Negotiators are representing the interests of an individual or a collective and so they will emphasise the strength of their case. They will often begin by saying that they are unwilling to move from their initial negotiating position.
Reaching outcomes to satisfy the interests of those involved	• For negotiation to be successful, an outcome needs to be reached that satisfies the interests of all those involved in the process. • After the differences between the parties have been explored, the aim of the negotiators is to reach an outcome that is broadly acceptable to each party in the negotiation process.

There are many different courses of action that can be used in the negotiation process:

- *Auction*: if a number of parties are involved, with competition between them, there may be a bidding process.

- *Brinkmanship*: this is where one party pushes another party to the edge or 'brink', making them think that they have no choice but to accept.

- *Deadlines*: the use of deadlines to force the other party to accept a decision.

- *Good guy/bad guy*: this can be used when teams are involved in the negotiation process, where one negotiator is seen as more reasonable than another.

 **Key term**

Negotiation: an interaction of influences that aims to reach an outcome that will satisfy the interests of those involved

Exam tip

Make sure you understand that the views and interests of as many stakeholders as possible should be taken into account in the process of negotiation.

◀ **Figure 1** *Setting the objectives of a negotiation*

Stages in the negotiation process

Planning the negotiation

Process	Explanation
Setting objectives	• The negotiator needs to be clear about the aims and objectives of the negotiation process so that he or she can stay focused on what is required. • It is important that the objectives of the negotiation process are SMART.
Choosing evidence to use	• The negotiator needs to make sure the appropriate and relevant information is collected so that it can be used in the negotiation. • Information should stand up to counter-argument from the other parties involved in the negotiation process.
Benefits of a proposal	• To be successful, a negotiator needs to be fully aware of the benefits and strengths of a particular position or argument.
Weaknesses of a proposal	• The negotiator needs to be fully aware of the possible weaknesses and limitations of any negotiating position in order to prepare an appropriate response if these weaknesses are raised by the other parties.
Arguments and counter-arguments for the proposal	• It will often be useful if a negotiator can 'win over' the other parties by explaining the potential benefits of accepting a particular proposal. • A negotiator may believe that the other parties should be fully aware of not only the potential benefits of accepting a proposal, but also the potential drawbacks. • It may be important to bring attention to the possible consequences of a proposal not being accepted. This may be part of the tactic of 'brinkmanship'.

▲ **Figure 2** *Negotiation in progress*

Conducting the negotiation

Process	Explanation
Setting the tone	• It is important that the negotiator sets an appropriate tone for the negotiation and that all of the negotiators are fully aware of how the discussions are going to proceed. For example, an agenda would outline the order in which issues will be discussed and how the meeting will proceed. Participants are then able to seek clarification on any issues. • Each side in the dispute should have an equal opportunity to present their case. The negotiator needs to consider the different ways of communicating within a process of negotiation, i.e. what kind of tone is going to be set. For example, a 'hard' or a 'soft' approach can be used. • The negotiator should consider the characters of the people involved in the negotiations, as this may influence the tone and negotiating style adopted.
Presenting the proposal	In terms of presenting the proposal, it is assumed that conflict resolution is based on a dual concern: • a concern for self, which stresses the importance of assertiveness • a concern for others, which stresses the importance of empathy. Different negotiating styles and strategies can be used to present a proposal, based on these two concerns, including the following: • *Accommodating*: negotiators are sensitive to the views and language of others involved in the negotiation process when presenting a proposal. • *Avoiding*: negotiators do not actually enjoy the process of negotiation, especially disagreement and confrontation, so they are more inclined to agree with others. • *Collaborating*: negotiators work constructively with others to solve problems in creative and imaginative ways. • *Competing*: negotiators enjoy the negotiation process and see it in terms of strategies to win rather than stressing the importance of relationships. • *Compromising*: negotiators are keen to bring the negotiation to an end, and so they are more willing to make concessions to enable a satisfactory agreement for all to be reached.
Understanding each other's point of view	• The needs, goals and interests of all parties at the meeting can be explored, and it is important to understand each other's point of view. • It may be useful to establish which needs and interests are more important than others, i.e. an order of priority can be established.
Summarising to check understanding	• It is important that the bargaining positions of each side are made very clear so that there are no misunderstandings between the parties. • Summaries of what has happened throughout the negotiating process can help to avoid misunderstandings, which could damage and undermine the process.
Reaching agreement	Before an agreement can be reached, each side puts forward their arguments as strongly as they can. • If the bargaining position is a 'hard' one, each side is determined to win at all costs, with no prospect of compromise – a 'win-lose' situation. • 'Soft' bargaining positions may be adopted so that all parties consider alternative strategies and possible compromises – a 'win-win' situation – where each side is willing to accept an outcome where they believe they have gained something positive. • The ultimate goal of any negotiation is the agreement, which needs to be clear so that both parties know exactly what has been decided. An appropriate course of action can then take place in order to implement the decision that has been reached. This may involve an action plan.

▲ **Figure 3** *Reaching agreement in a negotiation*

 Key term

Negotiating style: a particular approach to the process of negotiation

Exam tip

Make sure you understand the various elements involved in conducting the negotiation.

 **Apply**

Describe the main elements in the negotiation process.

 Review

It is important to understand the impact that negotiation skills can have on the success of a negotiation. The Student Book has a case study on Udemy, an organisation that offers courses in negotiation skills, on page 87. Some of the more important negotiating skills that the case study emphasises include presenting your arguments clearly, conducting negotiations with a diplomatic spirit and remaining calm throughout the negotiation process.

Measuring the success of a negotiation

Process	Explanation
What went well	It is important to review what went well in the negotiation process. These could include: • effective verbal communication • effective listening skills to reduce misunderstanding • building rapport to bring about strong working relationships between negotiators • demonstration of mutual respect • effective problem-solving skills • successful decision-making skills and techniques • assertiveness to show other negotiators that you feel strongly about something • ability to deal calmly and rationally with potentially difficult situations.
How to improve next time	There could be a number of ways that changes may be made in future negotiations, such as: • If confrontational, it might be useful to reappraise the approach taken, stressing the importance of using positive, non-confrontational language and looking for new options to resolve the dispute or conflict. It may also help if a negotiator speaks more calmly and slowly; this could indicate a move away from emotional to more rational behaviour. • The skill of active listening, as well as mutual respect and positivity, could be employed to create a greater degree of rapport and trust. This may make it easier for negotiators to provide insights into the reasons for their actions and demands – when these reasons are made clear, conflict resolution is easier to achieve. • When demands are high, negotiators can be unwilling to compromise or step down and the result can be a lose-lose outcome. A lowering of demands might be more helpful, not necessarily as a sign of a weaker position, but as a sign of collaboration and of working towards a 'win-win' situation.

 Recap

A negotiation process can involve:

• resolving disputes
• agreeing upon courses of action
• bargaining for individual or collective advantage
• reaching outcomes to satisfy the interests of those involved.

There are three stages in the negotiation process:

• planning the negotiation
• conducting the negotiation
• measuring the success of the outcome.

Sample question

1. **a.** Define the term 'negotiation'. [2]

   b. Explain why it is important to understand the weaknesses, as well as the benefits, of a negotiating proposal. [4]

   c. Analyse what is involved in reaching an agreement in a negotiation. [6]

   d. Discuss what is involved when the success of a negotiation is measured. [15]

Analysis

✓ In (a), you will need to clearly define what is meant by the term 'negotiation'.

✓ In (b), you will need to focus on providing an explanation of why it is important to understand the weaknesses, as well as the benefits, of a negotiating proposal.

✓ In (c), you will need to give a clear analysis of what is involved in reaching an agreement as part of the negotiation process.

✓ In (d), you will need to provide a clear discussion of what is involved when the success of a negotiation is being measured.

Mark scheme

a. One mark for stating that negotiation involves an interaction of influences that aims to reach an outcome; one mark for stating that the aim is to reach an outcome that will satisfy the interests of all those involved in the process.

b. Up to two marks for an explanation of the importance of understanding the benefits of a negotiating proposal; up to two marks for an explanation of the importance of understanding the weaknesses of a negotiating proposal.

c. Up to six marks for an analysis of what is involved in reaching an agreement as part of the negotiation process.

d. Knowledge and understanding, Level 1, 1–3 marks; some analysis, Level 2, 4–7 marks; good analysis, Level 3, 8–11 marks; clear reasoned evaluation, Level 4, 12–15 marks.

Student answer

(a) Negotiation can be defined as a process that involves a number of interested parties discussing different aspects of an issue or problem. [1 mark]

(b) Negotiators need to be fully aware of the benefits and strengths of a particular position or argument so that they can argue in favour of this position, giving them more chance of success. It will also be useful if the negotiator is fully aware of the possible limitations of any negotiating position. This awareness of the possible weaknesses of any negotiating position will enable the negotiator to anticipate these weaknesses by the other party. [3 marks]

(c) Sometimes an agreement is reached in a negotiation as a result of adopting a 'win-win' position, but this is not always the case. Sometimes a harder and more uncompromising negotiating position is adopted which can be described as a 'win-lose' position.   [2 marks]

(d) It is important to consider what is involved when the success of a negotiation is being measured. The elements that went well can be reviewed. For example, it could be that the verbal communication used throughout the negotiation process was clear and effective or it could be that confusion and misunderstanding were avoided by everybody listening carefully to what was being said. It could be that the working relationships between the different negotiators were respectful or it could be that potential problems were solved by the use of appropriate skills. It could be that the negotiators were very assertive in putting across their views and opinions.   [6 marks]

Total: 12 out of 27

✓ Examiner feedback

a. The candidate has made some attempt to define the term, pointing out that negotiation can be defined as a process that involves a number of interested parties discussing different aspects of an issue or problem, but the definition needed to be developed further by stressing that the aim of the negotiation process is to try and reach an outcome that will satisfy the interests of all those involved in the process.

b. The explanation is quite a reasonable effort, but could have been expanded upon in terms of being aware of the weaknesses of a negotiating position that would enable a negotiator not only to anticipate what might be said, but also to enable him or her to be able to respond in an appropriate way to such critical comments by the other party.

c. This is a rather limited response that could have gone much further. The distinction between a 'win-win' and a 'win-lose' position could have been made clearer by contrasting a 'soft' and a 'hard' negotiating position. If the bargaining position is a 'hard' one, it may well be that each party aims for a 'win-lose' situation, i.e. each side is determined to win at all costs, with no prospect of compromise.

However, 'soft' bargaining positions may be adopted so that all parties consider alternative strategies and possible compromises. In this situation, the parties can aim for a 'win-win' situation, i.e. each side is willing to accept an

outcome where they believe they have gained something positive as a result of the negotiation process. In such a situation, both sides believe that their point of view has been taken into account. Any agreement needs to be made absolutely clear so that both parties are aware of what has been decided as a result of the negotiation.

Once agreement has been reached, an appropriate course of action can then take place in order to implement the decision that has been reached. This may involve an action plan.

d. The candidate has made some useful comments on what may have gone well in the negotiating process, but there also needed to be a consideration of what could have been improved. For example, there could have been a change in the type of language used, such as a shift from threatening to non-threatening language or the use of a lower level of voice. Also, there could have been a greater degree of active listening in order to create a greater degree of trust.

Another approach could have been to lower demands. Sometimes, when demands are high, the result can be a lose-lose outcome when negotiators are unwilling to compromise or step down. It might have been more helpful if demands had been lowered, not necessarily as a sign of a weaker position, but as a sign of collaboration and of working towards a 'win-win' situation.

Unit 6:
Finance

Your exam

Finance is part of Component 1: Written Paper, and
Component 2: Coursework.

Component 1 is a 90-minute exam and makes up 50% of the total marks.
Component 2 is the coursework and makes up 50% of the total marks.

Your revision checklist

Tick these boxes to build a record of your revision

Specification	Theme	Tick
6.1 Sources of finance	Sources of start-up funding	
	Sources of funding for continuing trade and expansion	
6.2 The concept of trade credit	Trade credit	
6.3 Financial terms	Cash flow forecast	
	Break-even	
	Income statement	
6.4 Financial records	The purpose of financial records	
	How to prepare a cash flow forecast for an enterprise	
	How to prepare an income statement for an enterprise	

You need to know:

- the advantages and disadvantages of sources of start-up funding
- the advantages and disadvantages of sources of funding for continuing trade and expansion.

Sources of start-up funding

Source	Explanation	Advantages	Disadvantages
Personal savings (capital)	Use of the entrepreneur's personal savings (referred to as capital).	• The entrepreneur decides how to use the money. • If successful, he or she will get the money back.	• The amount of is likely to be relatively small. • If the enterprise fails, the money may be lost.
Family and friends	Funds from family and friends that could be in the form of a gift, but more likely as a loan.	• There is a low or even zero rate of interest. • Family and friends are likely to offer support.	• There may well be difficulties with family and friends if the money is lost.
Bank overdraft	Allowing an account to go into debit, usually up to a maximum amount.	• This is useful as a short-term source of funding. • It is easy to arrange.	• An agreed rate of interest will usually be paid. • Interest rates tend to be usually quite high.
Loans	An amount of money that is lent by a financial institution and needs to be repaid over an agreed period of time.	• Lower interest rates than overdraft but usually over a longer time period. • Larger amounts of money are usually available than an overdraft.	• An agreed rate of interest will usually be paid – this is the price of the loan. • The assets of the enterprise may be at risk if loan not repaid.
Leasing	A lease is when the lessee (the user) obtains the legal right to use an asset (e.g. a building or a vehicle) owned by the lessor in return for regular payments.	• This can be a good short-term financial arrangement. Also, the asset may be upgraded to a newer version.	• It may end up being more expensive than the cost of buying the asset.
Mortgage	A long-term loan that is usually linked to a property purchase, which provides security for the loan.	• The interest rate may be lower. • The amount that can be borrowed may be quite large.	• As a secured loan, the assets of an enterprise are at risk. • Detailed information of an enterprise will need to be given to obtain the mortgage.
Community sources, including charities and social enterprises	Sources of finance from the local community, such as charities and social enterprises (not-for-profit organisations).	• This brings money into the area. • Funds do not usually need to be paid back.	• The money usually has to be spent on a specified and mutually agreed project. • If it is not, the funds may be taken back.
Grants and subsidies	A government grant is a payment, usually to finance a specific project or service. A government subsidy is paid to an enterprise, to reduce the price charged to the customer.	• A grant does not usually need to be repaid. • A subsidy helps to keep down the costs of an enterprise.	• A grant usually needs to be spent on a specific project. • An enterprise may be required to meet certain criteria in order to be eligible for a subsidy.

Continued on next page

Source	Explanation	Advantages	Disadvantages
Crowdfunding	Raising finance by asking a relatively large number of people to each contribute a small amount of money. Uses the internet and social media.	• Individual investors only invest a relatively small amount of money, but this can lead to an enterprise raising a substantial amount of money.	• If an enterprise fails, investors will lose the money invested. • Not all enterprises are good at using the internet and social media to raise money.
Selling shares	The purchase of shares is more appropriate for expansion rather than start-up. It would be unusual for an enterprise to start as a limited company.	• Large amounts of money can be raised as large numbers of people may decide to purchase shares in an enterprise.	• Shareholders have a say in how an enterprise is run. • Those who originally started an enterprise may lose their majority of shares.

 Key terms

Building society: a financial institution that receives deposits and provides loans and other forms of financial support. It is usually owned by its members, and so is a mutual organisation

Commercial bank: a commercial institution that receives deposits and provides loans and other forms of financial support. It is usually owned by its shareholders

Credit union: a financial institution that receives deposits and provides loans and other forms of financial support. It is usually owned by its members, and so is a mutual organisation, but it tends to be limited to particular areas of a country or to particular groups of workers

Crowdfunding: the practice of funding an enterprise project or venture by raising small amounts of money from a large number of people, typically via the internet

Finance: the activities of an enterprise that are related to money

Friendly society: a financial institution that receives deposits and provides loans and other forms of financial support. It is usually owned by its members, and so is a mutual organisation. It is similar to a building society, but tends to be on a smaller scale, specialising in providing savings accounts and life insurance plans

Grant: a payment that is usually given to support a particular project or service

Interest: the return on money that has been lent or the payment for money that has been borrowed

Lease: a contractual arrangement whereby an asset is used for a specified period of time on payment of rent

Exam tip

Make sure you are able to clearly distinguish between a grant and a subsidy.

Exam tip

Make sure you understand what is distinctive about crowdfunding as a source of start-up funding. The idea is that a large number of people are able to invest relatively small amounts of money.

Common error

An overdraft, a loan, a lease and a mortgage are terms that are often confused. Make sure you are able to clearly distinguish between these four terms.

Key terms

Lessee: the person or organisation that rents an asset from a lessor

Lessor: the person or organisation that rents out an asset to a lessee

Loan: money that is lent by a financial institution to a borrower

Mortgage: a form of loan that is usually secured against a property

Overdraft: a situation when an account is allowed to go into debit

Share or **equity:** a contribution to the finance needed by an enterprise organised as a limited company; a share certificate is issued to the shareholder

Start-up: the beginning of an enterprise when it is first established

Subsidy: a payment that is usually given to keep the price charged to a consumer lower than would otherwise be the case

Exam tip

Make sure you understand the distinctive nature of venture capital in relation to enterprises that could be regarded as relatively risky.

Sources of funding for continuing trade and expansion

Source	Explanation	Advantages	Disadvantages
Personal savings (capital)	Could fund expansion of an enterprise, although funds not likely to be significant.	• The entrepreneur decides how to use the money. • If successful, he or she will get the money back.	• The amount of money is likely to be relatively small. • If the enterprise fails, the money may be lost.
Retained profit	Some profit could be reinvested, such as buying new equipment. How much depends on what is left after dividends have been paid to shareholders.	• Profits can be used without seeking approval (if there are no shareholders). • No interest needs to be paid.	• Shareholders need to give permission as retained profit will affect dividends. Shareholders may specify the ways profits should be used.
Private institutions	Private institutions (microfinance organisations) can be a source of funds.	• They can assist enterprises that cannot access more traditional financial institutions. • They can also provide money management courses.	• Interest will need to be paid on a loan, and this will sometimes be more than that charged by traditional financial institutions.
Venture capital	A collective investment which provides finance to enterprises that are regarded as relatively risky.	• Significant amounts of money can usually be raised. • Venture capitalists are experienced and can give an enterprise appropriate advice and guidance.	• Venture capitalists like to have a large say in how an enterprise is run. • This can sometimes lead to disagreement and conflict.
Issuing shares	Issuing shares is more appropriate for the expansion of an existing enterprise rather than for the creation of a new enterprise.	• Large amounts of money can be raised as large numbers of people may decide to purchase shares in an enterprise.	• Shareholders have a say in how an enterprise is run. • Those who originally started an enterprise may lose their majority of shares.

Recap

Sources of start-up funding include:

- personal savings
- family and friends
- financial institutions and the provision of overdraft, loan, lease and mortgage arrangements
- community sources, including charities and social enterprises
- grants and subsidies
- crowdfunding
- shares.

Sources of funding for continuing trade and expansion include:

- personal savings
- retained profit
- private institutions
- venture capital
- shares.

 Key terms

External sources of finance: funds that are found outside an enterprise

Internal sources of finance: funds that are obtained within an enterprise

Venture capital: a collective investment scheme designed to provide private equity capital for relatively small expanding enterprises

 Apply

1. Explain what is meant by a mortgage.
2. Describe the main features of venture capital.

 Review

There are advantages and disadvantages of the different possible sources of funding for an enterprise – what might be an appropriate source of funding for one enterprise may not be appropriate for another. Each enterprise is distinctive and so it is helpful to use case studies as illustrations.

On page 91 of the Student Book there is a case study of the Chilimba Saving and Investment Scheme in Zambia, which provides an informal grassroots means of saving for people in Zambia.

On page 94 of the Student Book there is a case study of how Kgalagadi Breweries Limited in Botswana provides grants to enterprises as part of its commitment to supporting sustainable enterprise development.

 Common error

Internal and external sources of finance are sometimes confused. Internal sources of finance are where funds are obtained within an enterprise, e.g. personal savings. External sources of finance are where funds are obtained outside an enterprise, e.g. venture capital.

Coursework tip

You will have the option to prepare financial planning materials for your enterprise project in Component 2: Coursework.

You need to know:

- the advantages and disadvantages of trade credit for entrepreneurs and suppliers (trade payables)
- the advantages and disadvantages of trade credit for entrepreneurs and customers (trade receivables).

Exam tip

Make sure you understand that credit arranged between entrepreneurs and suppliers is referred to as trade payables and that credit arranged between entrepreneurs and customers is known as trade receivables.

Trade credit

Trade credit is based on trust where enterprises may offer customers a period of time to make a payment – often 30, 60 or 90 days. The decision to offer credit depends on the reputation, reliability or creditworthiness of the customer. If a customer is regarded as being unreliable, credit may be denied.

Trade credit can also apply to the relationship between entrepreneurs and suppliers. The supplier may decide to allow the entrepreneur to have credit, i.e. payment is deferred for 30, 60 or 90 days.

The advantages and disadvantages of trade credit for entrepreneurs and customers

Advantages

- *For the enterprise (the creditor)*: the provision of credit by an enterprise may attract customers and repeat custom. For example, if one enterprise offers credit of 30 or 60 days, customers may be persuaded to buy from a rival enterprise offering 90 days' credit. This has the advantage of helping the enterprise to establish itself and possibly gain an increase in its market share. Trade credit can be regarded as a way of obtaining finance as the enterprise is providing the products without receiving immediate payment – a source of short-term, interest-free financing.

- *For the customer (the debtor)*: this credit period has the advantage that the customer has a relatively long time to make the payment. There is always an opportunity cost involved with any financial transaction and if a customer knows that payment does not have to be made for 90 days, that money can be used for other purposes.

Disadvantages

- *For the enterprise (the creditor)*: the extension of credit to as much as 90 days may affect cash flow. The firm demanding immediate payment may not be interested if the enterprise can pay in 90 days' time, as the firm will want payment now, not after 90 days.

- *For the customer (the debtor)*: the customer might have been able to pay when it purchased the goods, but it is possible that the customer experiences financial difficulties during the credit period and is then unable to pay.

Also, the customer may have been able to negotiate a discount for quick payment if payment had been immediate or within a short period of time and so the cost of goods to a firm may be higher as a result of using credit. When products are purchased and paid for at a later date, this is regarded as a short-term financial debt and is an example of a current liability.

The advantages and disadvantages of trade credit for entrepreneurs and suppliers

Advantages

- *For the enterprise (the creditor)*: trade credit will enable the enterprise to pay the supplier after products have been purchased by customers, by which time the enterprise will have received revenue from the sales.

- *For the supplier (the debtor)*: it may be wise not to insist on the enterprise making immediate payment because the enterprise could decide to make contact with an alternative supplier that was willing to provide a credit arrangement. Trade credit therefore encourages repeat custom.

Disadvantages

- *For the enterprise (the creditor)*: if the enterprise is unable to pay within the required number of days, penalties may be imposed, e.g. an increase in the amount of money owed.

- *For the supplier (the debtor)*: trade credit given by the supplier to the enterprise could have a disadvantage, especially in relation to cash flow, because the supplier may not receive the money owed for 90 days.

 Common error

The terms 'credit' and 'debt', and 'creditor' and 'debtor' are sometimes confused. Make sure you are able to clearly distinguish between a creditor and a debtor and between credit and debt.

 Recap

Trade credit has both advantages and disadvantages for:

- entrepreneurs and customers

- entrepreneurs and suppliers.

 Apply

Distinguish between trade receivables and trade payables.

 Key terms

Credit: a sum of money that a supplier allows an entrepreneur before requiring payment, and/or a sum of money that an enterprise allows a customer before requiring payment

Creditor: a person or organisation that is owed money

Debt: a sum of money that is owed by a person or organisation

Debtor: a person or organisation that owes money

Trade credit: the credit extended by a seller to the purchaser of goods and services

Trade payables: money owed by an enterprise to suppliers

Trade receivables: money owed by customers to an enterprise

 Review

It is important that you understand the meaning of trade credit and its various advantages and disadvantages for entrepreneurs, customers and suppliers.

An entrepreneur, customer or supplier may not have the funds available to make an immediate payment. So, over the years, credit has been important in allowing trade and enterprise to flourish by allowing a period of time before a payment needs to be made.

You need to know:
- about cash flow forecasts
- what break-even means
- what an income statement (profit and loss account) is.

Key terms

Break-even: the break-even point is when the total revenue of an enterprise exactly matches the total costs and the enterprise is not making either a profit or a loss

Cash flow: the inflow of money into and the outflow of money out of an enterprise

Cash inflows: cash flowing into an enterprise as receipts, e.g. from the money received from selling goods or services

Cash outflows: cash flowing out of an enterprise as payments, e.g. to pay employees and suppliers

Deficit: the amount by which an enterprise's expenditure or spending exceeds its income over a particular period of time

Fixed costs: the costs of an enterprise that do not vary directly with changes in the level of output

Net cash flow: the difference between money coming into, and of, an enterprise; it can either be a surplus or a deficit

Solvency: the degree to which the current assets of an enterprise are greater than its current liabilities

Surplus: the amount by which an enterprise's income exceeds its expenditure or spending over a particular period of time

Total costs: the total costs of an enterprise are made up of variable costs and fixed costs

Variable costs: the costs of an enterprise that vary directly with changes in the level of output

Cash flow forecast

- Cash flow refers to the movement of money into (inflow) and out of (outflow) an enterprise.
- It is usually measured over a specific period of time.
- An enterprise will want to have an idea of the amount of money that flows in and out and to achieve this objective it will create a cash flow forecast.

The significance of an enterprise having a cash flow deficit or surplus

- *Cash flow deficit*: an enterprise with a cash flow deficit could go bankrupt, even if it was profitable. If this is a short-term difficulty, which can be put right through borrowing, then the situation of insolvency may not last very long. However, if the insolvency continues in the long term, the enterprise may become bankrupt and will be forced to close. As long as an enterprise has a positive cash flow, it will be able to ensure that creditors, employees and suppliers can be paid on time.

- *Cash flow surplus*: a cash flow surplus is crucial to the survival of an enterprise – this surplus will mean that an enterprise will be able to support its operations and will be able to pay its creditors, employees and suppliers. This means that an enterprise is solvent and is likely to continue in existence for a relatively long period of time.

Break-even

Break-even analysis involves calculating the minimum level of sales required to cover the total costs of an enterprise – when the total revenue of an enterprise exactly equals the total costs of an enterprise and the enterprise is neither making a profit nor a loss. If the enterprise increases sales beyond this point, it will be making a profit.

The break-even point of an enterprise can be calculated by drawing a graph showing how variable costs, fixed costs, total costs and total revenue change with output.

A break-even graph or chart is constructed in the following way:

- The horizontal axis is labelled to show different levels of production or output or sales.

- The vertical axis is labelled to show the total costs. The fixed costs are shown by a horizontal line because they do not change with output, e.g. rent, interest and insurance. The variable costs, e.g. materials and energy, are shown by a straight line.

- The vertical axis is also labelled to show total revenue. This is the total amount of money received from selling the products and is calculated by multiplying the number of units sold by the price per unit.

The limitations of a break-even chart

Break-even analysis is a useful tool for calculating the minimum sales needed to avoid making a loss. However, it has a number of limitations:

- It is not always easy to estimate costs.

- It assumes that all units are sold.

- It assumes that forecasts are reliable.

- It assumes that the external environment in which the enterprise operates is stable.

Break-even analysis makes a number of assumptions, which may not always be accurate:

- Costs can change quickly, especially the variable costs, e.g. the cost of labour and/or raw materials may suddenly change.

- If a new enterprise enters a market or there is an economic recession, it could take longer for an enterprise to reach the break-even point than expected. Many enterprises add on a margin of safety when deciding on the minimum sales target.

Exam tip

Establishing the break-even point helps an enterprise to plan the levels of production it needs to be profitable

Contribution

Contribution is the difference between sales revenue and variable costs:

- If contributions are just enough to cover fixed costs, an enterprise breaks even.

- If contributions are less than fixed costs, an enterprise makes a loss.

- If contributions are greater than fixed costs, an enterprise makes a profit.

Contributions provide a fund out of which total fixed costs must be paid before any profit is made by an enterprise.

Income statement

An income statement (also known as a profit and loss account) refers to an income and expenses statement that shows the sales revenue of an enterprise over a period of time, usually 3 or 12 months, and all of the relevant costs. It is a statement of the financial performance of an enterprise during a particular period and shows the revenue and expenses of an enterprise.

An income statement shows how the sales revenue of an enterprise (before expenses are taken out) is turned into a net income (after expenses are taken out). This net income can also be termed the net profit of an enterprise.

 Common error

A cash flow surplus does not necessarily mean that an enterprise makes a profit – profit and cash flow are very different. A cash flow surplus simply means that there is more money coming into an enterprise than leaving it. Profitability takes into account the total income and the total expenditure of an enterprise.

 Key terms

Contribution: the difference between sales revenue and variable costs

Expenditure or **spending:** all of the outgoings of an enterprise over a specific period of time

Gross profit: the sales revenue of an enterprise less the cost of sales

Income: all of the incomings of an enterprise received from different sources over a specific period of time

Income statement or **profit and loss account:** a statement that shows the net profit of an enterprise after all of the expenses have been deducted

Loss: the gap or shortfall between an enterprise's sales revenues and the total costs incurred in producing the output of the enterprise

Net profit: the gross profit of an enterprise less all other expenses

Profit: the difference between the sales revenue and the total costs of an enterprise

Revenue: the income received from the sales of goods and/or services of an enterprise over a specific period of time

Income statement compared with a cash flow forecast

There are a number of differences between cash flow forecast and an income statement:

- A cash flow forecast shows the cash balance of an enterprise, whereas an income statement indicates whether an enterprise has made a profit over the trading period.

- The profit of an enterprise may not be the same as the cash received, such as when credit has been extended to purchasers.

- An enterprise may receive cash in one trading period from sales made in a previous trading period, which would increase the cash balance of an enterprise, but not its profit.

- An enterprise may borrow money, which would increase the cash balance, but have no effect on the profit of the enterprise.

- Purchases of fixed assets, such as machinery, will reduce the cash balance of an enterprise, but have no effect on its profit. Similarly, sales of fixed assets will increase the cash balance of an enterprise, but again have no effect on its profit.

- The amount of cash that an enterprise has at the end of a trading period will not be the same as the profit of the enterprise because it is unlikely that the cash balance of an enterprise will be zero at the beginning of the trading period.

Common error

A profit and loss account and a cash flow forecast are sometimes confused. Make sure you understand, and can explain, the difference between profit and loss and cash flow.

Recap

Three important financial terms are:

- cash flow forecast
- break-even
- income statement.

Apply

1. Explain the importance of an income statement to an enterprise.

2. Explain, using examples of each, the distinction between fixed costs and variable costs.

Review

You must clearly understand the meaning of a cash flow forecast, break-even analysis and an income statement or profit and loss account – these terms are very important in the financial operation of an enterprise. These financial aspects of the work of an enterprise are absolutely crucial to its continued success, as it is possible for a profitable enterprise to go bankrupt because of negative cash flow.

The preparation of a simple budget, including a cash flow forecast and an income statement, is covered in the next section.

You need to know:
- the purpose of income statements and budgets
- the reasons for keeping accurate financial records
- how to prepare a simple budget, including a cash flow forecast and an income statement.

The purpose of financial records

The purpose of a budget

An enterprise will draw up a budget for a number of possible reasons. It can:

- identify where expenditure may need to be controlled and reduced

- draw attention to the possible inefficiency of an enterprise

- clarify what an enterprise needs to do to improve its financial situation

- help an enterprise to establish specific and clear financial targets.

Budget variances

A variance is the difference between the budgeted figure and the actual figure. Variances are usually calculated at the end of the budget period when the actual figure will be known.

A favourable variance is when the actual figure is better than the budgeted figure; an adverse variance is when the actual figure is worse than the budget figure.

The purpose of an income statement

An enterprise will draw up an income statement for a number of possible reasons. It can:

- help people, such as creditors and investors, determine the past financial performance of an enterprise

- help to predict the future financial performance of an enterprise

- help to assess the capability of an enterprise to generate future cash flows through an understanding of its income and expenses

- show the ability of an enterprise to generate profit during a trading period, and how the size of this profit could be changed by increasing revenue and/or reducing costs

- show how an enterprise has controlled its overheads over a trading period

- be used to indicate the growth of an enterprise.

 **Key terms**

Budget: a financial statement of income and expenditure prior to a particular period of time

Budget variance: the difference between a budgeted or anticipated figure and the actual figure

Exam tip

Make sure you fully understand the meanings of the terms that are usually found in a budget.

Cash flow forecast: a forecast of expected income and expenditure over a particular period of time

Liquidity: the ease with which the assets of an enterprise can be turned into cash

Exam tip

Make sure you understand, and are able to explain, why a profitable enterprise may go bankrupt.

The purpose of a cash flow forecast

A cash flow forecast predicts what is likely to happen to an enterprise in the short term. This is useful for several reasons:

- It helps to determine the value or rate of return of a particular project or of all the work of an enterprise.
- It helps to give an indication of the financial strength of an enterprise, e.g. whether it is likely to have a surplus or a deficit in the near future.
- It helps to determine whether there are problems and difficulties with the liquidity of an enterprise. An enterprise may be making a profit, but this does not mean that it is liquid, i.e. its assets may not be in the form of cash or be able to be easily and quickly converted into cash.
- It helps an enterprise to evaluate the risks attached to the production of a particular product.
- It helps to identify poor decisions taken by the management and to assist in the planning and decision-making, e.g. whether additional workers should be employed or new equipment should be purchased.
- It helps to create performance targets for different sections and departments in an enterprise.
- It helps to set budgets for activities and projects of an enterprise.

Cash flow problems can come about in various ways:

- The enterprise has reached the limit of its overdraft.
- The enterprise is owed a lot of money by purchasers who have taken advantage of the provision of trade credit.
- The enterprise owes money to the tax authorities.
- The enterprise owes money in the form of rent.
- The enterprise does not have a working capital buffer, i.e. it is literally operating from day to day.

Reasons for keeping accurate financial records

- *The need to provide a true and fair view to stakeholders:* accurate financial records show how much income is being generated by an enterprise, how much is being spent and what the money is being spent on. Accurate and up-to-date financial records can indicate the strengths and weaknesses of an enterprise and how changes could be made to improve its efficiency and profitability.

  For example, if an enterprise is organised as a limited company, accurate and up-to-date financial records are required if prospective investors are going to be attracted to buy shares. Accurate financial records will be needed in order to calculate the dividends to be paid to the shareholders in the event of making a profit.

- *Legal and taxation purposes:* an enterprise may be legally required to keep accurate financial records. For example, a limited company is legally required to keep certain financial records. Enterprises need to submit a tax return to show what the tax implications of its operation are, and if audited for tax purposes, accurate and up-to-date financial records are particularly important.

- *Forecasting:* future income and expenditure can be projected, and regularly reviewed, from the financial records in order to give an enterprise the necessary focus and direction. This will give an indication of what changes in an enterprise need to be made.

  Accurate financial records help an enterprise to know whether there will be enough cash to meet its financial commitments, such as wages, and make it easier to produce a cash flow forecast to show whether the incomings are sufficient to cover the outgoings..

- *Decision-making for owners/shareholders:* accurate financial records are essential if an enterprise approaches a financial institution for a loan. The potential lender will need to see the records in order to make a judgment about the financial health of the enterprise.

  The financial records will also be used to inform the business plan, or any revisions of a business plan, which will indicate how any loan will be used by the enterprise.

Key term

Shareholder: an individual who contributes funds to a limited company in return for shares in the company

How to prepare a cash flow forecast for an enterprise

A cash flow forecast includes all the necessary information relating to cash inflow and cash outflow.

The cash inflow would include the 'revenue stream' that would change a cash account over a given period of time. Cash inflows into an enterprise are generated in one of three ways:

- financing
- operations
- investing.

The cash outflow would include the 'expenses stream' that would change a cash account over a period of time. Cash outflows from an enterprise are generated in one of two ways:

- expenses
- investments.

The following table shows a cash flow forecast for an enterprise for three months.

Item	First month	Second month	Third month
Opening bank balance	$2500	$1500	–$1500
Total receipts (money in)	$500	$1000	$6000
Total spending (money out)	$1500	$4000	$2000
Closing bank balance	$1500	–$1500	$2500

An enterprise can improve its cash flow by:

- reducing cash outflows, e.g. by delaying the payment of bills or securing better trade credit terms
- increasing cash inflows, e.g. by selling assets or by obtaining an overdraft.

Key terms

Gross profit: the sales revenue of an enterprise less the cost of sales

Net profit: the gross profit of an enterprise less all other expenses

Exam tip

You will need to be able to make financial calculations in relation to the pre-released case study.

Exam tip

Make sure you know, and can explain, the difference between gross profit and net profit. Gross profit is the sales revenue of an enterprise less the cost of sales. Net profit is the gross profit of an enterprise less all other expenses.

How to prepare an income statement for an enterprise

An income statement includes all the necessary information relating to revenue and expenses. The revenue would include all cash inflows into the enterprise as a result of its operations. This is essentially the sales revenue or gross revenue before the deduction of expenses.

The cash outflow would include:

- the expenses involved in producing an enterprise's output, known as the cost of sales
- the expenses involved in the selling and distribution of products
- the depreciation of assets of an enterprise
- expenses involved as a result of research and development
- tax expenses
- interest expenses.

The following table shows an income statement for an enterprise.

Sales revenue	$100 000
Less cost of sales	$60 000
Gross profit	$40 000
Less other expenses	$25 000
Net profit	$15 000

 Recap

- You should understand the purpose of income statements and budgets, including cash flow forecasts.
- You should understand the reasons for an enterprise keeping accurate financial records.
- You should know how to prepare a simple budget, including a cash flow forecast, and an income statement for an enterprise.

 Apply

Describe the purpose of a cash flow forecast.

 Review

Accurate financial records are very important in the operation of an enterprise.

There is a case study of the Flame of Africa enterprise on page 107 of the Student Book, which illustrates the importance of keeping such records. The managers of this enterprise, in particular, stress the importance of producing accurate cash flow forecasts, taking into account changes in economic conditions in different countries.

Sample question

1. **a.** Distinguish between a 'loan' and an 'overdraft' as ways of an enterprise obtaining start-up funding. [2]

      b. Describe **two** advantages of trade credit for an enterprise. [4]

      c. Explain the benefits and limitations of break-even analysis for an enterprise. [6]

      d. Analyse the possible reasons for an enterprise to keep accurate financial records. [10]

Analysis

✓ In (a), you will need to clearly distinguish between a loan and an overdraft as ways of an enterprise obtaining start-up funding.

✓ In (b), you will need to accurately describe two advantages of trade credit for an enterprise.

✓ In (c), you will need to explain the benefits and limitations of break-even analysis for an enterprise.

✓ In (d), you will need to analyse, and not just describe, the possible reasons for an enterprise to keep accurate financial records.

Mark scheme

a. One mark for explaining the meaning of a loan as a way of obtaining funding; one mark for explaining the meaning of an overdraft as a way of obtaining funding, making it clear how it is different from a loan.

b. Up to two marks for a description of each of two advantages of trade credit for an enterprise, such as the fact that it may attract customers and repeat custom; it may also help to establish an enterprise and possibly improve its market position; it is also a way of obtaining finance and it has the advantage of giving an enterprise the opportunity to pay back money after the revenue from sales has been received.

c. Up to three marks for an explanation of the benefits of break-even analysis for an enterprise; up to three marks for an explanation of the limitations.

d. Knowledge and understanding, Level 1, 1–3 marks; some analysis, Level 2, 4–7 marks; good analysis, Level 3, 8–10 marks.

Student Answer

(a) A loan involves an enterprise borrowing a certain sum of money over a period of time whereas an overdraft is simply an arrangement whereby a financial institution allows an enterprise to take out more than is in an account, up to a specified limit. An overdraft is therefore a form of short-term borrowing whereas a loan is more of a long-term borrowing.   [2 marks]

(b) One advantage of trade credit for an enterprise is that by offering it to a customer, it could help to attract customers and repeat custom. Another advantage is that by obtaining it from a supplier, payment can be made at a later date after sales revenue has been received.   [2 marks]

(c) Break-even analysis has a number of benefits for an enterprise. It involves the calculation of the minimum level of sales required to cover the total costs of an enterprise. It can therefore show, at low levels of sales, that an enterprise is not selling enough units for revenue to cover its costs and that a loss will be made. The break-even point is reached when the total revenue of an enterprise exactly equals the total costs of an enterprise and this will show that the enterprise is not making a profit or a loss. Break-even analysis will show that if an enterprise increases sales beyond this point, it will be making a profit. It is therefore extremely useful in helping an enterprise avoid making a loss and indicating what will need to be done to make a profit.   [3 marks]

(d) An enterprise keeps accurate financial records for two main reasons. Firstly, there is a need to provide a true and fair view of the financial affairs of an enterprise to the various stakeholders. For example, stakeholders will need to know how much income is being generated by an enterprise, how much is being spent and on what the money is being spent. The records will give an indication of the financial strengths and weaknesses of an enterprise and may help to show what could be done to improve its efficiency and profitability. A shareholder is an example of a stakeholder and the records will help to calculate the dividend that will need to be paid to a shareholder. A second reason for keeping financial records is for legal and taxation purposes. An enterprise may be required by law to keep accurate records. An enterprise will also need to submit a tax return and so accurate records will be useful in working out how much tax an enterprise will need to pay. If an enterprise is being audited for tax reasons, the records will be very important.   [5 marks]

Total: 12 out of 22

Examiner feedback

a. The candidate has clearly distinguished between the two ways of obtaining start-up funding for an enterprise and has gained both marks.

b. The candidate has identified two advantages of trade credit for an enterprise, but has not really explained them in any depth.

The explanation of the first advantage could have been developed more fully by pointing out that customers would be attracted to the enterprise by the provision of trade credit, especially if other enterprises did not offer this, giving the enterprise a competitive advantage.

The explanation of the second advantage could have been expanded by pointing out that this situation would be particularly useful in terms of cash flow.

c. The candidate has made quite a reasonable effort to explain the benefits of break-even analysis for an enterprise, but needed to expand on the answer by including an explanation of possible limitations. For example, it is not always easy to estimate costs, as they may change quickly, especially variable costs such as the costs of labour materials.

There is also an assumption that all units produced will be sold, but this will not necessarily be the case. It is also assumed that the forecasts are reliable, but again this may not be the case, especially if there are major changes in the external environment, such as a recession.

d. The candidate has analysed two possible reasons for an enterprise to keep accurate financial records, but there were two other reasons that could also have been brought into the answer.

One of these is that forecasting and keeping accurate records can help give an enterprise focus and direction, showing what changes might need to be made. Accurate financial records will help an enterprise produce a cash flow forecast and such a forecast would be helpful in indicating whether it might be necessary to increase income and/or reduce expenditure.

Another possible reason for an enterprise to keep accurate financial records would be in relation to decision-making in the enterprise. For example, accurate financial records would be necessary if a decision was made to apply to a financial institution for a loan.

Financial records would also help an enterprise to update its business plan as, if a loan was applied for, it is almost certain that the financial institution would want to see the business plan of the enterprise.

Unit 7:
Business planning

Your exam

Business planning is part of Component 1: Written Paper, and Component 2: Coursework.

Component 1 is a 90-minute exam and makes up 50% of the total marks.
Component 2 is the coursework and makes up 50% of the total marks.

Your revision checklist

Tick these boxes to build a record of your revision

Specification	Theme	Tick
7.1 Business objectives	Aims and objectives of enterprises	
	The influence of aims and objectives on enterprises	
7.2 Action plans	The purpose and importance of action plans	
	The contents of action plans	
	Methods of monitoring action plans	
	The importance of updating action plans	
7.3 Business plans	The purpose and importance of business plans	
	The contents of business plans	
	Methods of monitoring business plans	
	The reasons for updating business plans	

- **that objectives are short term and aims are long term**
- **that enterprises have a range of objectives.**

Aims and objectives of enterprises

It is important to recognise that aims and objectives relate to different time periods, although there are no precise and universally agreed definitions of the particular periods of time:

- *Short-term* objectives are often seen within the context of the operational planning of an enterprise and this is likely to be for a period of, perhaps, three to six months, but it could extend to be as long as a year.

- *Long-term* aims can be seen within the context of the broader strategic planning of an enterprise and this is likely to be for a longer period of two, three or five years.

The objectives of enterprises

Objective	Explanation
Ethical, not-for-profit, social, belief-based	• Ethical aims and objectives are linked with the concept of social responsibility. • Many enterprises operate in a socially responsible way towards such stakeholders as customers, employees, suppliers and the local community. For example, an enterprise may be a not-for-profit organisation with social and community objectives. • An enterprise may have wider goals that relate to the environment, e.g. an enterprise might wish to be seen as environmentally friendly based on reducing the level of pollution. This may require good relations with relevant pressure groups, such as Friends of the Earth and Greenpeace.
Legal compliance	• One objective of an enterprise is to comply with current laws and regulations relating to how it is set up and operated. • It needs to ensure that contracts or agreements are legally binding and meet the necessary requirements. • An enterprise must comply fully with health and safety laws and regulations. Failure to do so may result in a fine or even the possibility of being closed down by the legal authorities.
Profit	• The main objective of many enterprises is not just profit, but profit maximisation, i.e. to make the gap between total revenue and total cost as great as possible. • However, an enterprise may have the objective of satisficing – the profit of an enterprise is sufficient to please the stakeholders, but could be greater. • Profit is not the main objective of not-for-profit social enterprises.

Continued on next page

Key terms

Aim: an overall general goal that an enterprise wants to achieve in the long term

Objective: a specific target that an enterprise wants to achieve in the short term

Exam tip

You need to understand that objectives relate to the short-term and that aims relate to the long-term.

Exam tip

Although there are no agreed definitions of the length of such time periods as the short-term and the long-term, you need to understand the importance of them in relation to the planning of an enterprise.

Common error

Candidates sometimes confuse a business enterprise and a social enterprise. Make sure you understand the difference between them.

▲ **Figure 1** *Demonstration by a pressure group about the use of different sources of energy and an enterprise's objectives and behaviour*

Exam tip

Make sure you understand that profit is the difference between the revenue and costs of an enterprise.

Exam tip

Make sure you understand what is meant by the term 'satisficing' and you appreciate how it can affect how an enterprise behaves.

Exam tip

Make sure you can demonstrate that you understand the difference between profit maximisation and a satisfactory level of profit.

Exam tip

Make sure you can clearly distinguish between the internal and external growth of an enterprise.

 Common error

Profit maximisation and sales revenue maximisation are not the same. Make sure you understand the difference between these two objectives.

 Common error

Some candidates seem to believe that profit maximisation is the goal of every enterprise, but there are many that do not aim to make a profit.

Objective	Explanation
Sales revenue	• Maximising sales revenue is an alternative goal for an enterprise that wishes to expand its market share.
	• The level of production needed to generate profit maximisation will not necessarily be the same as that needed to generate sales revenue maximisation.
	• There are two ways to increase the profits of an enterprise: increasing sales revenue and decreasing total costs.
	• Sales revenue (income from sales) could be increased by raising the price of products if the demand is not very sensitive to a price change. If demand is sensitive to a price change, revenue may be increased by lowering the price of the products.
	• Advertising can also be used to increase sales revenue by increasing the awareness of the products.
Cash flow	• Positive cash flow is essential to the solvency of an enterprise.
	• If enough cash is immediately available, an enterprise can pay creditors, employees and suppliers on time.
	• If there is not enough cash immediately available, it will not be able to support its operations and could become insolvent.
	• If the cash flow deficit is a short-term difficulty, then insolvency may not last for very long.
	• If the insolvency continues in the long term, the enterprise may become bankrupt and go out of business.
Growth	• An important objective of an enterprise may be internal and/or external growth.
	• Internal growth refers to the expansion of an enterprise through increasing sales, e.g. through an increase in the number of outlets (shops or factories).
	• External growth refers to the expansion of an enterprise through taking over, or merging with, other enterprises, with the aim of increasing sales. It may also reduce costs, contributing to increased profits.
Survival	• A common objective of many enterprises, especially in the early years, is survival. An entrepreneur may lack experience and resources and face stiff competition from established enterprises in a market.
	• Survival is a logical aim in its early years.

The influence of aims and objectives on enterprises

The aims and objectives will affect how an enterprise operates. For example, if an enterprise wishes to increase its profit, it will need to increase its sales revenue and/or reduce its costs. However, a reduction in costs could be as a result of taking decisions that could damage the environment.

Similarly, reducing costs could lead to it behaving in an unethical way, such as in relation to the payments made to employees and suppliers. The growth of an enterprise may help it to increase sales revenue and reduce costs, but if this is as a result of taking over another enterprise, some workers could lose their jobs.

Maximising growth may be one of a number of important objectives that an enterprise may have, but it should not be at the expense of other objectives, such as its ethical behaviour, product quality or environmental impact.

 Recap

- Objectives are relatively short term and aims are relatively long term.

- Enterprises can have different aims and objectives. Examples are aims and objectives based on not-for-profit status, social issues, organisational beliefs, legal compliance, profit, sales revenue, cash flow, growth and survival.

- Aims and objectives can influence the activities of enterprises.

 Apply

Distinguish between profit maximisation and sales revenue maximisation.

 Key terms

Growth: the increase in size of an enterprise through internal and/or external expansion

Legal compliance: the process or procedure to ensure that an enterprise follows relevant laws, rules and regulations

Profit maximisation: the goal of many enterprises to make the gap between total revenue and total cost as wide as possible

Sales revenue maximisation: where an enterprise aims to maximise the revenue received from sales rather than its profit

Satisficing: where an enterprise aims for an adequate level of profit, rather than profit maximisation

Social responsibility: the idea that an enterprise has a responsibility towards the wider society and environment

Review

It is important that you have a clear understanding of the aims and objectives of enterprises. The aims and objectives of an enterprise can influence its activities. One example is an organisation's promotion of healthy eating in schools, ensuring that children can choose a healthy diet. There is a case study about healthy eating on page 115 of the Student Book.

You need to know:
- the purpose and importance of action plans
- the contents of action plans
- the methods of monitoring action plans
- the importance of updating action plans.

Key term

Action plan: a plan that outlines the actions required to achieve particular aims and objectives and which provides a way of monitoring progress

The purpose and importance of action plans

An action plan:

- is a detailed framework outlining the various actions that need to be taken to reach particular aims and objectives

- allows managers to monitor progress, allowing them to handle projects efficiently

- establishes the steps needed to achieve the end goal, e.g. it outlines each of the tasks that will need to be carried out

- will contribute to the establishment of a bond within an enterprise, as each member is aware of his or her individual role in achieving the success of a project

- can also help to create motivation and keep members focused on what they are aiming to achieve.

The contents of action plans

An action plan:

- will contain a sequence of steps that need to be taken for a strategy to be successful

- will outline the various tasks that need to be undertaken and the amount of time that will need to be spent on each task, with a set date for completion

- will contain important information about the aims and objectives of a project and will set targets. These targets will need to be SMART (specific, measurable, achievable, realistic, time-based). Specific roles and appropriate resources will then need to be allocated.

Methods of monitoring action plans

- The success of an action plan can be monitored by analysing the progress achieved in relation to certain targets and by ensuring that tasks have been completed efficiently and by the agreed deadline.

- As a result of the monitoring process, it may become necessary to make some changes to the action plan and so it is important that it is regularly updated.

The importance of updating action plans

- Although many threats and opportunities will have been identified in the production of an action plan, it is not possible to predict everything with certainty.

- It is important to update an action plan, especially to take account of any challenges or threats that may have emerged since the beginning of the project.

Exam tip

Answers to the following key questions form the six stages of an action plan:

- What are the key activities or tasks?

- When must the key activities or tasks take place and how long will they take to complete?

- Who is responsible for carrying out the key activities or tasks?

- By what date does each key activity or task have to be completed?

- As the key activities or tasks are carried out, how will progress be monitored?

- Once the key activities and tasks have been completed, what is the outcome?

 Coursework tip

You will be required to produce an action plan for your enterprise project in Component 2: Coursework.

 Recap

You will need to know:

- the purpose and importance of action plans

- the contents of action plans

- the methods of monitoring action plans

- the importance of updating action plans.

Apply

Describe the purpose and importance of action plans.

 Review

You need to understand the purpose and importance of action plans – their contents, the possible methods of monitoring them and the importance of updating them. An action plan is fundamental to the success of an enterprise because it outlines the actions required for an enterprise to achieve its aims and objectives.

Action plans need to be effectively executed if they are to have any value to an enterprise. There is a case study illustrating the effective execution of an action plan, through a step-by-step approach, by the enterprise ViRTUS on page 117 of the Student Book.

Key term

Business plan: a document that summarises the main aims and objectives of an enterprise and how these are to be achieved

Exam tip

Make sure you clearly understand what is meant by a business plan.

Exam tip

All business plans will be slightly different, but they are usually broadly similar. Make sure you understand what is likely to be included.

Exam tip

Make sure you understand the possible reasons why an enterprise might want to draw up a business plan.

The purpose and importance of business plans

- A business plan is a statement, usually contained in a formal document, that outlines the purpose of an enterprise and how it will try to achieve its aims and objectives.

- There are a number of reasons why an enterprise would want to draw up a business plan. A business plan is important:

  o to present to a financial institution when seeking to negotiate a loan

  o to give a clear idea of its direction to all stakeholders

  o to outline how it is going to operate

  o to anticipate potential problems and so minimise the risk of something going wrong.

- There is usually an element of risk when people lend money and so potential investors need to be convinced that the enterprise is well-organised and focused on what it needs to do to achieve its aims and objectives. A business plan will clearly establish these aims and objectives, and indicate how they are going to be achieved.

The contents of business plans

The business plans of two enterprises will not be exactly the same as each other, but there are likely to be broad similarities. Each will be likely to contain the following information:

- *The enterprise:* the name and address of the enterprise, its aims and objectives and the type of organisation.

- *The product:* the good being produced and/or the service being offered, the quantity of products and the proposed price.

- *Marketing or the market:* the results of market research and analysis conducted by the enterprise, the anticipated size of the market, the rate of growth of the market, likely demand, strengths and weaknesses of the competition and methods of promotion and advertising.

- *Personnel or human resources:* who will be involved in the enterprise and their skills and experience.

- *Production and operations:* the method of production and costs of production.

- *Premises and equipment:* the type, location and cost of premises and the type and age of equipment.

- *Finance:* the expected profit, the break-even point, cash flow forecast, how much money will be put in to the enterprise by the owners and how much money will need to be borrowed.

Methods of monitoring business plans

- A business plan can be a useful tool for monitoring the operations of an enterprise.
- An effective tracking system needs to be developed so that particular goals and targets in a business plan can be checked, e.g. cash flow, profitability, market share, actual and potential competition and marketing strategies.
- Forecasts and projections can be compared with actual outcomes to judge how successfully the enterprise has been operating.

The reasons for updating business plans

- A business plan is very important to an enterprise, both when the enterprise starts up and when it is well established.
- Economic circumstances can change and there may be a decrease in the demand for an enterprise's products. It is therefore important to regularly update the business plan to incorporate any changes.
- There may also be changes in the size of the market, or in the rate of growth of the market or in relation to the competition.
- A business plan is likely to include information about the type of business organisation, which may change over a period of time, e.g. an enterprise may start as a sole trader but may eventually become a partnership.
- Financial institutions are only likely to consider a loan if the enterprise's business plan is up to date.

 Recap

You will need to know:

- the purpose and importance of business plans
- the contents of business plans
- the methods of monitoring business plans
- the reasons for updating business plans.

 Apply

Explain why a business plan needs to be regularly updated.

 Review

You need to understand the purpose and importance of business plans – their contents, the possible methods of monitoring them and the importance of updating them. A business plan can play a key role in the success of an enterprise because it summarises the main objectives of an enterprise and how these objectives can be achieved. There is a case study about the enterprise Pact, focusing on the importance of a business plan, on page 119 of the Student Book. It stresses the importance of a detailed business plan in helping to persuade investors to invest in Pact.

Exam tip

Make sure you understand that to monitor a business plan effectively it will be necessary to obtain and analyse a variety of information, such as:

- marketing or the market e.g. changes in market share
- personnel or human resources data, e.g. changes in the number of employees
- production and operations data, e.g. total output produced by an enterprise
- finance data, e.g. cash flow.

Exam tip

You need to understand that once a business plan has been produced, it remains important and will need to be updated on a regular basis.

Sample question

1. **a.** Distinguish between an objective and an aim of an enterprise.   [2]

   b. Explain the importance of updating action plans.   [4]

   c. Describe the likely contents of a business plan.   [6]

   d. Analyse the importance of a business plan for an enterprise just starting up.   [10]

Analysis

✓ In (a), you will need to clearly distinguish between an objective and an aim of an enterprise, particularly in relation to the time period.

✓ In (b), you will need to clearly explain the importance of updating an action plan used by an enterprise.

✓ In (c), you will need to accurately describe the likely contents of a business plan produced by an enterprise.

✓ In (d), you will need to give a clear analysis of the importance of a business plan at the start-up stage of an enterprise.

Mark scheme

a. One mark for explaining the meaning of an objective of an enterprise; one mark for explaining the meaning of an aim of an enterprise, making it clear how it is different from an objective, especially regarding timescale.

b. Up to four marks for a clear explanation of the importance of updating action plans to take account of any challenges or threats that may have emerged since the beginning of the enterprise project.

c. Up to six marks for a description of the contents of a business plan of an enterprise, such as the name and address of the enterprise, its aims and objectives, the type of organisation, the product, the market, personnel, methods and costs of production, premises and equipment and finance.

d. Knowledge and understanding, Level 1, 1–3 marks; some analysis, Level 2, 4–7 marks; good analysis, Level 3, 8–10 marks.

Student answer

(a) An aim is an overall general goal and an objective is a specific target. [1 mark]

(b) Action plans need to be updated on a regular basis so that they can take account of changes that may have taken place since the beginning of the enterprise project. [1 mark]

(c) Business plans vary, but they are likely to contain information about the name and address of an enterprise and about its main aims and objectives. A business plan is also likely to contain information about the product, e.g. whether it is a good or a service, and about the price that will be charged for the product. A business plan is also likely to include information about the market in which an enterprise is operating. For example, the findings of market research are likely to be included and information such as the anticipated size of the market, the rate of growth of the market, the likely demand for the product, the strengths and weaknesses of the competition and information about methods of promotion and advertising. [3 marks]

(d) A business plan will be very important for an enterprise that is just starting up because it will outline the ways in which an enterprise will try to achieve its aims and objectives. It will set out what the purpose of the enterprise is and how it plans to be a success. There are two important reasons why an enterprise would want to draw up a business plan. Firstly, it can be shown to a financial institution when negotiating a loan, in an attempt to convince the institution that it is an enterprise that will be capable of repaying the loan. Secondly, it will help to give a focus and sense of direction to all stakeholders involved in the enterprise. [5 marks]

Total: 10 out of 22

 Examiner feedback

a. The candidate has attempted to distinguish between an aim and an objective of an enterprise, but the answer needed to be developed more fully by pointing out that objectives are short term and aims are long term.

b. The candidate has made a brief comment on why it is important to update action plans, but the answer could usefully be expanded. For example, there is a general reference to changes but no examples are given. The candidate could have referred to particular challenges or threats, e.g. problems in obtaining the necessary parts and materials or in obtaining staff with the required skills and experience. Updating an action plan gives an opportunity to review what has happened and if any problems have emerged, then the action plan can be adapted and modified to take account of any problems.

c. The candidate has made some attempt to describe the likely contents of a business plan, especially in areas such as the enterprise, the product and the market. However, the candidate could have gone further by describing other likely features of a business plan, such as in relation to personnel (e.g. the skills and experience of the workforce), production (e.g. the methods and costs of production), premises and equipment (e.g. the type and age of the equipment to be used), and finance (e.g. the expected profit, the break-even point, a cash flow forecast and how much money might need to be borrowed).

d. The candidate has analysed a number of reasons why a business plan would be useful for a start-up enterprise, especially in relation to applying for a loan and in relation to giving the enterprise a sense of direction, but there were other reasons that could also have been considered. For example, a business plan could outline how the enterprise is going to operate and it could also try and anticipate possible problems in the future, so minimising the risk of something going wrong that might threaten the future existence of the enterprise.

Unit 8:
Markets and customers

Your exam

Markets and customers is part of Component 1: Written Paper, and Component 2: Coursework.

Component 1 is a 90-minute exam and makes up 50% of the total marks.
Component 2 is the coursework and makes up 50% of the total marks.

Your revision checklist

Tick these boxes to build a record of your revision

Specification	Theme	Tick
8.1 The purpose of marketing	Marketing to achieve enterprise aims	
	Marketing from the perspective of customers	
8.2 Market research	Methods of identifying potential customers	
	The effectiveness of market research methods for different enterprises	
8.3 Customer retention	The reasons for retaining customers	
	The methods of measuring customer satisfaction and retention	
	The methods of retaining existing customers	
8.4 Marketing communications	The mass media	
	Selecting appropriate methods for different enterprises	

You need to know:
- how marketing increases consumer awareness of the enterprise and its products, establishes and maintains brand loyalty, affects sales, market share or profit
- how marketing enables customers to make more informed decisions.

Marketing to achieve enterprise aims

The meaning of marketing

- Marketing is the communication of information, about the enterprise and also its products, to potential and existing customers, in order to influence their behaviour.

- Marketing is the process of identifying, anticipating and satisfying the needs and requirements of consumers profitably.

- Marketing has been described as the process involved in getting the right product at the right price to the right place at the right time.

Benefits of marketing

Increasing consumer awareness of the enterprise or product

- Marketing makes consumers aware of what an enterprise stands for and what it sells. Marketing should reflect the aims and objectives of an enterprise and should try to aid their achievement, e.g. if an enterprise stresses the importance of ethical considerations and/or corporate social responsibility, marketing needs to ensure that consumers are aware of this.

- Marketing increases consumer awareness of the existence of an enterprise and its products (goods and services). Where there is intense competition, marketing must stress the particular features and characteristics of an enterprise's products from those of another enterprise. One way of achieving this is to emphasise the brand identity of particular products.

Establishing and maintaining brand loyalty

- Branding aims to clearly differentiate one product from another in order to make it distinctive to consumers. An effective brand name needs to be relatively easy to remember. It should also project the image of the enterprise and the positive features and characteristics of the product. A brand is not only identified through a name or image, but also through a symbol, logo or trademark.

- Emphasising a brand name is part of a strategy to establish and maintain brand loyalty. Consumers often have a high degree of loyalty to a particular brand and a strong brand identity will help one enterprise to appear different from another. For many consumers, loyalty to a particular brand is associated with identification with a particular brand image.

Increasing or defending sales, market share or profit

A marketing objective would help to achieve the aim to increase an enterprise's:

- total sales, either by value of sales or by volume of sales, or by both

- market share, and possibly to gain the leadership of a market

- profits over a particular period of time.

 Key terms

Brand: a name or image that clearly distinguishes one product from another

Branding: the strategy of differentiating the products of one enterprise from those of another through emphasising an identifiable image

Brand loyalty: the degree to which consumers buy a particular brand of a product in preference to another brand

Marketing: the process of communicating relevant information in order to influence the behaviour of consumers in ways that will benefit an enterprise

Marketing strategy: a long-term plan devised in order to achieve particular marketing objectives

Key term

Consumer sovereignty: the importance of changes in consumer preferences in determining the allocation of scarce resources in an economy

▲ **Figure 1** *It is important that customers make an informed choice when choosing products*

Marketing from the perspective of customers

There are two potential benefits for a customer of marketing.

Greater knowledge of the enterprise or product

- Decision-making by customers will be strongly influenced by the knowledge they possess. Rational and logical decisions to purchase something will be constrained if there is a lack of information and knowledge.

- If customers are in possession of a wide range of knowledge, they will be able to make a more informed choice. Marketing will assist customers in making a decision, as they will have greater knowledge about what is available in a particular market.

The ability to make more informed decisions

- The informed customer is at the heart of consumer sovereignty, i.e. the idea that it is consumer demand that determines the allocation of scarce resources in an economy, and it is likely that an informed customer will be able to make better choices between alternatives. Marketing plays a key role in helping to make customers more informed than would otherwise be the case.

- Marketing can make a customer better informed about the range of enterprises and products that exist in a market, saving a great deal of time. It would take a long time for a customer to find out information about the range of enterprises and products on offer.

 Recap

Marketing can help to achieve enterprise aims through:

- increasing consumer awareness of the enterprise and its products
- establishing and maintaining brand loyalty
- increasing or defending sales, market share or profit.

Marketing can help to achieve customer aims through:

- greater knowledge of the enterprise and its products
- increasing the ability of customers to make more informed decisions.

 Apply

Explain what is meant by branding.

Review

Marketing is of fundamental importance to an enterprise by establishing and maintaining brand loyalty, and also to its customers by helping them make more informed choices. Marketing is concerned with different ways in which the behaviour of consumers can be influenced in ways that will benefit an enterprise.

Market research is covered in the next section.

You need to know:
- about primary and secondary market research
- the advantages and disadvantages of each method in terms of cost, availability, suitability for the enterprise and the suitability for reaching the potential target market.

Methods of identifying potential customers

- An entrepreneur will need to identify the need or want for a product, i.e. if there is a gap in the market for a particular product. This indicates a customer or market (rather than a producer or supply) orientation, and gives the enterprise a customer focus.

- It is not enough that an entrepreneur thinks that he or she has a wonderful idea for a new product; the demand for such a product needs to be established, otherwise the enterprise may fail.

- It will therefore be necessary to conduct market research to establish whether demand for a particular product actually exists.

Market research refers to the collection and analysis of information about a particular market. There are essentially two ways of carrying out research and collecting information – primary research and secondary research.

Primary research

Primary research is first-hand research and involves asking people questions about particular products – these people might be existing customers or potential customers or retailers. Primary research is sometimes called field research and it involves finding out information that does not already exist.

Primary research can include a variety of different methods, including:

- questionnaires
- personal interviews
- telephone interviews
- postal surveys
- online surveys

- observation
- focus groups
- consumer panels
- test marketing.

Primary research can be further classified as quantitative or qualitative research:

- *Quantitative research* involves gaining information that is capable of being analysed in terms of hard factual data, e.g. a certain percentage of a population is likely to buy a particular product at a certain price.

- *Qualitative research* involves gaining information that is of a softer, more subjective nature, e.g. people's attitudes towards, or opinions about, a particular product.

Secondary research

Secondary research is second-hand research (sometimes called desk research) and involves making effective use of information that already exists. Information that is obtained from within an enterprise is known as *internal* research, and information obtained from outside an enterprise is known as *external* research.

Common error

Make sure you understand the difference between quantitative and qualitative research.

Exam tip

You must understand the difference between primary research and secondary research.

Exam tip

Make sure you understand the differences between a want and a need and between a market orientation and a producer orientation.

 Key terms

Field research: ways of gaining first-hand information through such methods as a questionnaire or an interview

Market orientation: an approach where an enterprise takes decisions on the basis of consumer demand

Market research: the collection and analysis of information that relates to the consumption of goods or services

Need: an item that is essential for survival

Primary research: the collection of information that does not already exist through different forms of field research

Qualitative research: the gaining of information in the form of soft subjective data, e.g. opinions and attitudes

Quantitative research: the gaining of information in the form of hard objective data, e.g. statistics

Want: an item that is desirable, but not essential

Key terms

Desk research: the ways of gaining second-hand information through such methods as analysing sales figures from inside an enterprise or using government research reports from outside the enterprise

Secondary research: the collection of information that already exists through different forms of desk research

Exam tip

The effectiveness of particular market research methods will depend on the relevant local context of each enterprise.

Apply

Explain, with the use of examples, the distinction between internal and external secondary market research.

Review

Market research, both primary and secondary, is extremely useful in identifying potential customers and in achieving the objective of maximising the number of customers. Once market research has helped an enterprise to gain as many customers as possible, it will need to focus on how to retain these customers. Customer retention is discussed in the next section.

Internal sources of information can include:

- existing market research reports
- sales figures
- reports from the sales teams
- complaints from customers who have bought products
- the Annual Report and Annual Accounts of an enterprise
- information from the website of an enterprise
- share movements (if an enterprise is organised as a limited company).

External sources of information can include:

- information from competing enterprises
- government publications and research reports
- publications from a regional economic body
- international publications, such as from the World Bank
- newspaper and magazine articles and reports
- trade or industry publications.

The effectiveness of market research methods for different enterprises

- *Cost:* primary research is particularly useful with a new product, but it tends to be expensive. Secondary research is generally cheaper as the information has already been collected.

- *Availability:* it may be the case that no secondary information has been collected on a particular product, or it could be that the information collected is out of date and no longer relevant.

- *Suitability for the enterprise:* some methods of market research may be more suitable for one enterprise than another, e.g. personal interviews can provide useful information to an enterprise, but there is always the possibility that interviewees have not been honest in their answers.

- *Suitability for reaching the potential target market:* one research method may be more suitable for reaching the potential target market than another, e.g. an online survey will be more useful to an enterprise that is planning to sell its products mainly through the internet than a more general survey.

Recap

There are two main types of market research method of identifying potential customers:

- primary research
- secondary research.

The effectiveness of various methods of market research for different enterprises will depend on their:

- cost
- availability
- suitability for the enterprise
- suitability for reaching the potential target market.

You need to know:
- how to retain customers through brand loyalty, increasing or defending sales, market share or profit
- how to measure customer satisfaction and retention
- methods used to retain existing customers.

The reasons for retaining customers

It takes much more time, effort and expense to gain new customers that it does to retain existing ones. It is therefore crucial for an enterprise to ensure a high level of customer satisfaction as retaining customers will be critical to its success.

- *Establishing and maintaining brand loyalty*: an enterprise needs to make sure it gives its customers good reasons to stay loyal, otherwise its competitors will give them various reasons to leave. It is important to establish and maintain brand loyalty; if customers are loyal to a brand, they will be more likely to keep using an enterprise.

- *Increasing or defending sales, market share or profit*: customer retention is critical to the success of an enterprise in terms of its sales, market share or profit. If customers are satisfied, it is much more likely that they will return for repeat, follow-on, business without considering the possibility of transferring to a competitor.

The methods of measuring customer satisfaction and retention

Customer satisfaction is an essential objective in retaining existing consumers; this is especially the case where there is a great deal of competition in a market.

Customer satisfaction is one of a number of key performance indicators that can be useful in managing and monitoring the success of an enterprise. It can be measured in the following ways:

- *The number of sales and complaints*: the number of sales, especially the trend in sales, can indicate the level of customer satisfaction, and so can the number of customer complaints.

- *Mystery shopper feedback questionnaires*: a mystery shopper is a person who is employed by a market research company to measure quality of service and to gather specific information about products in order to produce a feedback questionnaire on what was discovered. The enterprise is unaware it is being examined.

- *Focus groups:* these are small groups of people whose reactions and opinions are studied as part of the market research process.

 Key terms

Customer retention: the degree to which customers are loyal to an enterprise and are likely to buy its products again in the future

Customer satisfaction: the degree to which the products supplied by an enterprise, and the quality of the service provided in selling those products, meet or exceed the expectations of customers

Focus group: a small number of people who are brought together to give feedback on a specific good or service

Mystery shopper: a person employed by a market research firm to visit retail establishments, posing as a casual shopper, to collect information on products and the quality of service

▲ **Figure 2** *Enterprises often have sales of reduced-price products to attract and retain customers*

The methods of retaining existing customers

There are a number of ways of retaining existing customers, including the following:

- *Effective customer service*: an enterprise needs to demonstrate that it knows its customers, and makes them feel valued through its quality of service. Its staff should dress appropriately and be trained to communicate positively and effectively with customers.

- *Resolving complaints*: an enterprise should be able to deal with complaints so that a resolution can be reached in the most mutually acceptable way. Complaints need to be taken seriously and efforts made to understand their cause. Any apology should be sincere, without blaming a particular person in the enterprise. Resolution of the grievance may offer appropriate compensation, to make sure the customer retains a positive opinion of the enterprise.

- *Loyalty rewards*: an enterprise can establish a reward or loyalty scheme, such as by giving 'money off' deals to regular customers, which can make them feel a part of the enterprise and encourage them to return.

- *New products*: an enterprise will be better able to retain existing customers if it can offer them new products or if it can have regular promotions, such as '10% off all products' or 'buy one get one free' offers, or have regular sales of products to attract customers.

- *Other possible methods*: customers can be asked for their opinions about the enterprise through a survey, and a prize can be offered to a lucky respondent; customers can be kept informed about the enterprise and its products, such as through a newsletter or a leaflet.

 Apply

Explain why it is important for an enterprise to establish and maintain brand loyalty.

 Review

You need to understand that it takes much more time, effort and expense for an enterprise to gain new customers than it does to retain existing ones. There are a number of methods that can be used to retain existing customers, such as effective customer service, loyalty rewards and the introduction of new products. Marketing communications will be covered in the next section.

 Recap

These are reasons why an enterprise should try to retain customers:

- It takes much more time, effort and expense to gain new customers that it does to retain existing ones.
- Competitors will not be able to benefit if the enterprise can retain its customers by establishing and maintaining brand loyalty.
- Retaining customers is a way to increase or defend sales, market share or profit.

Methods of measuring customer satisfaction and retention include:

- the number of sales and complaints
- mystery shopper feedback questionnaires
- focus groups.

Methods of retaining existing customers include:

- effective customer service
- resolving complaints
- loyalty rewards
- new products.

You need to know:
- methods of marketing communication to reach intended customers
- which methods of marketing communication are appropriate for different enterprises
- advantages and disadvantages of different methods.

The mass media

The mass media is a general term for a number of different possible methods of communicating with a market for different types of enterprise, including television, radio, cinema, newspapers and magazines.

Television

- Television is available all over the world and the development of digital television has expanded the number of television channels that are available, so enterprises can reach many more people in order to promote their products.

- As a means of communicating with a market, television can be very expensive, so only larger enterprises are likely to use national or international television channels. However, local and regional television channels are likely to be cheaper than national and international channels and more appropriate for an enterprise's needs.

Radio

- Radio is also available in countries all over the world. Using radio for marketing purposes is cheaper than using television. As with television, the development of digital radio has increased the number of available stations.

- Although there are many national radio stations, there is more of a tradition of local radio than local television, so using local radio for marketing is likely to be relatively cost-effective for even small- and medium-sized enterprises, especially those whose market is concentrated in particular areas of a country.

Cinema

- The availability of cinemas will vary greatly from one country to another and even within one country.

- Cinema may, therefore, not be an appropriate method of communicating with a market for many enterprises, although it may be useful to advertise in a cinema if there is one local to the enterprise.

Newspapers and magazines

- All countries will have a range of local, regional and national newspapers and magazines that could be used by an enterprise to communicate with a market.

- If the activities of an enterprise are national in scope, newspapers and magazines may be an appropriate method to communicate with its market. However, it is usually the case that newspapers and magazines are read by a particular market segment, such as a particular social class. If an enterprise promotes its products in one of these, it will need to check that the advertisement is reaching its intended or target audience.

- Local and/or regional newspapers and magazines may be more appropriate for small- and medium-sized enterprises although, again, an enterprise will need to consider whether advertisements are reaching its intended or target audience.

 Key term

Mass media: a mixture of various technologies that are used to reach an audience

Posters and leaflets

Posters

- Posters usually have a good visual impact. They exist in all countries and can be placed in a variety of different locations throughout a country.

- Posters are likely to be more effective for a small- or medium-sized enterprise if they are displayed in particular towns or regions. Of course, if a larger enterprise is national in the scope of its operations, a national poster campaign could be an effective form of communicating with a market.

Leaflets

- Whereas a poster is usually a stationary form of promotion (although they can be put on the side of buses and other forms of transportation), a leaflet is smaller and can be handed out to potential customers in particular areas.

- Leaflets are relatively cheap to produce, so they are likely to be a cost-effective method of communicating with a market for a small- and medium-sized enterprise that is located in a particular area.

Online communication and social media

Website

- Most enterprises will have their own website. This will involve obtaining an internet service provider, buying or renting a website name, designing and installing the website graphics and other functions (such as a means of taking orders), promoting the website (such as through various search engines and directories) and maintaining the website.

- Websites are an increasingly important method of communicating with a market. They are relatively cost-effective and easy to update. In many markets, an enterprise will be at a disadvantage compared with its competitors if it does not have a website. For example, if an enterprise is aiming at the international market, the use of a website for prospective customers to place orders in different countries is absolutely vital to the success of such an objective.

Email

- Many, if not all, enterprises, ask their existing and potential customers to give them their email address. It is then able to provide these customers with information, such as special offers and new products.

- This form of communication is a very cost-effective method for an enterprise to communicate with its customers and so is appropriate for any enterprise, whatever its size.

Internet advertising

- As well as having its own website, an enterprise can also advertise itself and its products on the internet.

- This method of advertising can be quite expensive and so is more appropriate for larger enterprises.

Social media

- Many enterprises use social media platforms to promote themselves and their products. Examples of social media include Twitter, Facebook, Linkedin, Whatsapp and Instagram.

- Social media marketing gives an enterprise a great opportunity to communicate directly with its existing and potential customers.

▲ **Figure 3** *Enterprises can use newspapers and magazines to distribute 'money off' coupons*

Key terms

Social media: websites, other online means of communication and applications that enable users to share information and to participate in social networking

Target audience: a particular group of people who are identified as the intended recipient of an advertisement or message

Website: a set of web pages served from a single web domain; all publicly accessible websites collectively comprise the World Wide Web

Word of mouth and announcements

Word of mouth

- Word of mouth is one of the oldest, and certainly the cheapest, methods of communication. An enterprise can build up a good reputation simply through customers telling people how good a particular enterprise is.

- A positive reaction by customers, and a willingness to tell others about this experience, can be crucial to the success of an enterprise, especially in the early start-up phase.

Announcements

- An announcement is where an enterprise makes a formal statement about an occurrence or an intention, e.g. an enterprise could make an announcement about the opening of a new store or about an extension of the opening hours of an existing store.

Sponsorship

- Sponsorship is where an enterprise supports an event or an organisation financially, through the provision of either funds or goods and services. It benefits from the association of the name of the enterprise with the particular event or activity.

- Some forms of sponsorship can involve vast sums of money. However, sponsorship at a local level can involve modest sums of money, which would provide financial assistance to an event and also gain publicity as a result.

Selecting appropriate methods for different enterprises

Each method of marketing communication has various advantages and disadvantages:

- *Cost*: television is likely to be a more expensive method of communication than radio. Posters and leaflets are likely to be relatively inexpensive and word of mouth will require no cost at all.

- *Availability*: cinema may not be available in all countries, or at least not in all parts of a country. This would influence an enterprise in deciding whether to use cinema as a method of communication or not. Local newspapers will be cheaper than national newspapers, but not all areas of a country will necessarily have a local newspaper.

- *Suitability for the enterprise*: one method of marketing communication may be more suitable for one enterprise than another, e.g. a local enterprise with one store deciding to extend its opening hours may simply decide to make a local announcement, whereas a much larger enterprise may decide to use television to make the public aware of something.

- *Suitability for reaching the potential target market*: an enterprise may decide to use different forms of social media, such as Facebook or Twitter, to reach a particular target market.

 Key terms

Announcement: a public and typically formal statement about a particular occurrence or intention

Sponsorship: a situation where an enterprise supports an event or an organisation in some way and receives publicity as a result

Word of mouth: people speaking to each other about a particular enterprise

Exam tip

The effectiveness of particular methods of marketing communication will depend on the relevant local context of each enterprise.

 Coursework tip

You have the option to produce marketing communications for your enterprise project.

Recap

The different methods of marketing communication to reach intended customers include:

- television, radio, cinema, newspapers and magazines
- posters and leaflets
- online communication and social media
- word of mouth and announcements
- sponsorship.

Selection of appropriate methods of marketing communication for different enterprises will depend on the advantages and disadvantages of each method in terms of:

- cost
- availability
- suitability for the enterprise
- suitability for reaching the potential target market.

 Apply

Explain the potential usefulness of posters for an enterprise wishing to communicate with intended customers.

 Review

There are many different forms of marketing communications, such as through the mass media, the internet, social media and word of mouth.

Case studies can illustrate how particular enterprises use different marketing communications methods to good effect. There is a case study about the Mr Stanford enterprise on pages 135–136 of the Student Book, which stresses how the company's website helps to establish its distinctive brand name.

Page 137 of the Student Book has a case study on the potential importance of word of mouth as a method of marketing communication for the Raft Floating Restaurant, Botswana. It illustrates how word of mouth can operate – satisfied customers tell others of their positive experience at the restaurant and also summarise their experiences in reviews that can be posted on social media and on the internet.

1. **a.** Define the term 'marketing'. [2]

    b. Explain, with the use of examples, the difference between primary research and secondary research. [4]

    c. Analyse the potential contribution of mystery shoppers and focus groups to the measurement of customer satisfaction. [6]

    d. Discuss the extent to which an enterprise should make use of the mass media in communicating with its intended customers. [15]

Analysis

✓ In (a), you will need to clearly define what is meant by the term 'marketing'.

✓ In (b), you will need to explain the difference between primary research and secondary research, using appropriate examples of each to support the explanation.

✓ In (c), you will need to give a clear analysis of the potential contribution of two groups to the measurement of customer satisfaction: mystery shoppers and focus groups.

✓ In (d), you will need to provide a clear discussion of the extent to which an enterprise should make use of the mass media in communicating with its intended customers, taking into account the various advantages and disadvantages of the different forms of mass media.

Mark scheme

a. One mark for explaining the meaning of marketing as a process of communicating relevant information; one mark for emphasising the purpose of marketing in influencing the behaviour of consumers in ways that will benefit an enterprise.

b. Up to two marks for an explanation of primary research, using appropriate examples to support the explanation; up to two marks for an explanation of secondary research, using appropriate examples to support the explanation and making it absolutely clear how the two methods of research are different.

c. Up to three marks for an analysis of the potential contribution of mystery shoppers to the measurement of the level of customer satisfaction by an enterprise; up to three marks for an analysis of the potential contribution of focus groups to the measurement of the level of customer satisfaction by an enterprise.

d. Knowledge and understanding, Level 1, 1–3 marks; some analysis, Level 2, 4–7 marks; good analysis, Level 3, 8–11 marks; clear reasoned evaluation, Level 4, 12–15 marks.

Student answer

(a) Marketing refers to the process of communicating information between the sellers and the buyers of a product.   [1 mark]

(b) Primary research refers to the collection of original information through field research. Secondary research refers to the collection of information that already exists through desk research.   [2 marks]

(c) A mystery shopper is a person employed by a market research organisation to visit enterprises and to collect information on products and the quality of service. The mystery shopper then gives feedback on what he or she has discovered and this will provide very useful data that, when analysed, can give an enterprise a very good idea of the level of customer satisfaction with the enterprise in general and with its products in particular.   [3 marks]

(d) An enterprise could make extensive use of the mass media in communicating with its intended customers, but the different forms of media may have particular advantages and disadvantages. Television can reach a large number of people and will be likely to attract a lot of interest and attention, but television advertising is relatively expensive when compared with other possible methods, so only very large enterprises are likely to be able to afford it. Advertising in newspapers, especially local ones, may be more useful and will be much cheaper than using television. Magazines may be particularly suitable because they are often very specialised and so will be useful for an enterprise aiming to communicate with a particular target market.   [6 marks]

Total: 12 out of 27

 Examiner feedback

a. The candidate has pointed out that marketing refers to the process of communicating information between the sellers and the buyers of a product, but there is no reference to the fact that the purpose of marketing is to influence the behaviour of consumers in ways that will benefit an enterprise.

b. The candidate has explained the difference between primary research and secondary research, but has made no reference to any examples of each approach. Examples of primary research could have been brought in to the answer, such as questionnaires, interviews, surveys and observation. Examples of secondary research could have been brought in to show the distinction between internal research, such as through existing market research reports, and external research, such as through information obtained from government reports.

c. The candidate has made a reasonable attempt to analyse the potential contribution of mystery shoppers to the measurement of customer satisfaction, but there is no reference at all to the potential contribution of focus groups. The candidate could have explained that a focus group refers to a small number of people who are brought together to give feedback on a specific good or service. They can express the views and opinions of typical customers and build up a picture of what consumers think about an enterprise and its products.

d. The candidate has made some useful comments on television, newspapers and magazines, but there is no reference at all to radio or cinema. Advertising on radio is likely to be much cheaper than on television and advertising on a local radio station will be very appropriate for an enterprise that only operates in a relatively small area. Not all countries have an extensive network of cinemas, but if there is a cinema located in a community, an enterprise could use that to make people aware of its existence and its products.

Unit 9:
Help and support for enterprise

Your exam

Help and support for enterprise is part of Component 1: Written Paper, and Component 2: Coursework.

Component 1 is a 90-minute exam and makes up 50% of the total marks.
Component 2 is the coursework and makes up 50% of the total marks.

Your revision checklist

Tick these boxes to build a record of your revision

Specification	Theme	Tick
9.1 Sources of help and support	Formal sources of help and support	
	Informal sources of help and support	
	The suitability of different sources of help and support for an enterprise	

Formal sources of help and support

Government bodies

Government help and support to enterprise could include the following:

- Tax concessions could be given, especially to enterprises that are just starting up or are in their first year or two of operation.

- A government could ensure that courses in enterprise are included in the curriculum in schools and colleges.

- A government could provide financial support to enterprises, such as through the provision of grants and/or subsidies.

- A government could have a regional policy where aid and assistance is concentrated in particular areas, such as special economic free trade zones; enterprises that choose to locate in certain parts of a country could benefit from such assistance.

- A government could launch a campaign to provide information relating to the setting up and running of an enterprise; workshops and seminars could be organised to ensure that the relevant information was made available to those who could benefit from it, and there could also be an online information website.

- Empty and under-used government offices could be made available to enterprises to help them to start up and develop.

▲ **Figure 1** *A government could organise a seminar to support the setting up of enterprises*

Business and enterprise agencies

Different types of business and enterprise agencies include:

- start-up agencies
- Confederation of Industry
- Chamber of Commerce
- Institute of Directors
- Federation of Small Businesses
- Business Link
- Enterprise Link.

These agencies could be a useful source of help and support for enterprise by:

- providing appropriate information about the setting up of new enterprises

- organising meetings and conferences to which successful entrepreneurs could be invited; this would provide opportunities for them to talk about what they have done to achieve success

- providing mentoring and face-to-face consultation sessions.

Consultants

- A consultant is an expert or experienced professional in a specific field who has a wide knowledge of the subject matter.

- Consultants can be brought in by an enterprise to give advice on a particular aspect of enterprise activity, such as business planning, market research and financial advice.

Key terms

Consultant: a person who provides expert advice in a particular area of enterprise activity

Regional policy: a government policy that is designed to concentrate help and support in particular areas of a country

Financial institutions

- Financial institutions, such as banks, building societies, credit unions and friendly societies, often provide help and advice to entrepreneurs who have a business account with them. This guidance can be especially effective in relation to the financial aspects of starting up and running an enterprise.

- Financial institutions can give advice to help an enterprise produce an appropriate business plan.

- They can give financial support to enterprise organisations, e.g. through the provision of a loan (see Unit 6).

Charities

- Charities support enterprise start-up initiatives in many countries, e.g. in the UK, the Prince's Trust runs an Enterprise Programme.

- Charities can be very effective in providing help and support for enterprise.

Teachers

- Teachers in schools and colleges can be a valuable source of help and support by providing a range of assistance in different aspects of the work of an enterprise.

Business and enterprise networks

- They can be very effective forums for advice and discussion.

- They provide opportunities for people who share similar business and enterprise interests to come together to discuss mutual concerns.

- They enable new business relationships to be formed, giving people the opportunity to learn from the experiences of others.

- They can vary in terms of their formality – some can be very formal with meetings organised on a regular basis, while others may be less formal.

- They can help to set up an incubation centre as an appropriate environment for entrepreneurs to start up an enterprise.

Other entrepreneurs

- Other entrepreneurs can share their experiences with people who are thinking of starting up an enterprise. Contact with inspiring people can often be through business and enterprise networks.

- Some may be willing to act as a mentor by using their experience to offer useful and constructive advice.

- They will be enthusiastic and will want to share their knowledge and experience and may help a start-up entrepreneur to avoid some basic mistakes.

Prince's Trust

▲ **Figure 2** *The Prince's Trust has been operating its Enterprise Programme since 1976*

Key terms

Business and enterprise network: a means of bringing together people to share, and learn from, their experiences in business and enterprise

Incubation centre: a place where resources, space and an appropriate environment are provided for entrepreneurs to start up an enterprise

Mentor: an experienced person who will be a source of useful advice

Informal sources of help and support

Friends and peers

- Friends and peers may have experience of starting and running an enterprise and could offer help and support as well as advice relating to their own experiences of success and failure.

Family

- Family members can offer help and support, especially if they have had experience of running an enterprise.

The suitability of different sources of help and support for an enterprise

Different sources of help and support will be more suitable to some enterprises than others:

- A start-up enterprise, needing to borrow money, is likely to focus on financial institutions as a source of help and support.

- A start-up enterprise is also likely to benefit from the advice and guidance given by other entrepreneurs.

- A more established enterprise may need specialised assistance and consultants are likely to be able to provide suitable assistance in this respect.

 Recap

Formal sources of help and support for enterprise include:

- government agencies or business agencies
- consultants
- financial institutions
- charities
- teachers
- business networks
- other entrepreneurs.

Informal sources of help and support for enterprise include:

- friends and peers
- family.

 Review

It is important that you have a clear understanding of the different sources of formal and informal help and support for enterprises. Both new and established enterprises face uncertainties so it is advantageous if they can be helped by a variety of agencies and organisations. Case studies in the Student Book illustrate the suitability of these different sources of help and support: the Oxfordshire Local Enterprise Partnership, stressing the importance of enterprise and innovation (page 141); the Prince's Trust, emphasising the advantages of its enterprise programme (page 142); the Pune Business and Enterprise Network, stressing its role in bringing together entrepreneurs (page 143); Women's Business Networking in Hong Kong, stressing the importance of empowering women in enterprise initiatives (page 144); the Namibian entrepreneur Naomi Natangwe Kefas who has emphasised the need to involve more mentors in enterprise initiatives (page 144).

Apply

Explain how a mentor could be a useful source of help and support for a start-up enterprise.

Sample question

1. **a.** Distinguish, with the use of examples, between a formal and an informal source of help and support for an enterprise. **[2]**

   b. Explain **two** ways a government could help enterprise. **[4]**

   c. Analyse how a financial institution could be a source of help and support for an enterprise. **[6]**

   d. Discuss how a business and enterprise network could assist a start-up enterprise. **[10]**

Analysis

✓ In (a), you will need to clearly distinguish between a formal and an informal source of help and support for an enterprise, including appropriate examples of each.

✓ In (b), you will need to clearly explain two ways in which a government or government body could help enterprise.

✓ In (c), you will need to analyse different ways in which a financial institution could be a source of help and support for an enterprise.

✓ In (d), you will need to discuss the different ways in which a business and enterprise network could assist a start-up enterprise.

Mark scheme

a. One mark for explaining the meaning of a formal source of help and support for an enterprise, with an appropriate example; one mark for explaining the meaning of an informal source of help and support for an enterprise, with an appropriate example.

b. Up to two marks for each explanation of two ways a government could help enterprise, such as through tax concessions, the provision of grants and/or subsidies, the encouragement of enterprise as a subject in the curriculum and the provision of appropriate information relating to enterprise.

c. Up to six marks for an analysis of how a financial institution could be a source of help and support for an enterprise, such as through the provision of a loan, offering help and advice, especially in relation to financial matters, and assistance in the drawing up of a business plan.

d. Knowledge and understanding, Level 1, 1–3 marks; some analysis, Level 2, 4–7 marks; good analysis, Level 3, 8–10 marks.

Raise your grade

Student answer

(a) A formal source of help and support for an enterprise is one involving an institution or network that is bounded by certain rules and contracts. An informal source of help and support, on the other hand, is one that is less rigid and with fewer or no rules and contracts.   [1 mark]

(b) One way in which a government could help enterprise is through the provision of tax concessions. This would be particularly helpful for a start-up enterprise. A second way in which a government could help enterprise is through the provision of information that is relevant to the setting up and operation of an enterprise.   [2 marks]

(c) A financial institution, such as a bank, a building society, a credit union or a friendly society, could be a source of help and support for an enterprise in a number of different ways. One way could be in offering help and advice to entrepreneurs, providing guidance on a range of matters, especially those concerned with the financial aspects of enterprise. Another way could be in helping an enterprise produce an appropriate business plan.   [3 marks]

(d) A business and enterprise network could assist a start-up enterprise in many different ways. Members could provide information relevant to the start-up of an enterprise and they could organise meetings, conferences and seminars to which established entrepreneurs could be invited to give a speech about their enterprise experience. The idea is that all entrepreneurs can gain from listening to, and talking with, other entrepreneurs. It provides a networking platform where different people can exchange contact details.   [4 marks]

Total: 10 out of 22

✓ Examiner feedback

a. The candidate has clearly distinguished between a formal and an informal source of help and support for an enterprise, but has not included any examples. For example, government bodies and business and enterprise agencies are examples of formal sources of help and support and friends, peers and family are examples of informal sources of help and support.

b. The candidate has identified two ways a government could help enterprise, but neither has been explained in any depth. For example, there is a reference to tax concessions with a suggestion that this would be particularly helpful for a start-up enterprise, but there is no explanation as to why this would be the case. The candidate could have explained that this would enable an enterprise to reinvest more of the profit, making survival more likely. The candidate then suggests that a government could provide information that is relevant to the setting up and operation of an enterprise. But this needed to be developed more fully by suggesting what information in particular would be helpful, e.g. information on producing a business plan.

c. Again, the answer really needed to be developed more fully. For example, there is a reference to the provision of help and advice on financial matters, but none of these are specified. There could have been a reference to cash flow, break-even or an income statement. Another source of help and support, which is not referred to at all in the answer, is a financial institution, which could provide financial support to an enterprise in the form of a loan.

d. The candidate has made an attempt to discuss how a business and enterprise network could assist a start-up enterprise, but the answer needed to be developed more fully. For example, there is no reference to the fact that a business and enterprise network could assist in arranging a mentor for an enterprise – a new entrepreneur could learn a great deal from a more established entrepreneur. Also, there is a reference to a business and enterprise network providing a network platform, but there is no attempt to consider the potential advantages of networking.

Unit 10:
Communication

Your exam

Communication is part of Component 1: Written Paper, and Component 2: Coursework.

Component 1 is a 90-minute exam and makes up 50% of the total marks.
Component 2 is the coursework and makes up 50% of the total marks.

Your revision checklist

Tick these boxes to build a record of your revision

Specification	Theme	Tick
10.1 Types of communication	Formal and informal communication	
	Verbal and non-verbal communication	
	Appropriateness of different types of communication for communicating with internal stakeholders	
	Appropriateness of different types of communication for communicating with external stakeholders	
10.2 Meetings and presentations	Planning a meeting	
	Documents for meetings and presentations	
	The effectiveness of meetings or presentations	

You need to know:

- about formal and informal methods of communication
- about verbal and non-verbal methods of communication
- how body language affects communication
- the types of communication used to communicate with internal and external stakeholders.

Key terms

Formal communication: the official channels of communication used within an enterprise

Informal communication: the unofficial channels of communication used within an enterprise

Organisational structure: the particular way in which an enterprise is structured in order to perform its different activities

Coursework tip

You are required to write formal reports for your enterprise project.

▲ **Figure 1** *Communication can take different forms*

Formal and informal communication

Methods of communication within any enterprise can be formal or informal depending on the audience:

- *Formal communication* consists of messages that are sent and approved by an enterprise, such as writing a report for investors or potential investors or having an official business meeting.

- *Informal communication* consists of messages that are not formally approved by an enterprise, such as sending an email to a friend or talking to a friend at lunch.

Differences in language

Language used in communication will differ, depending on the context and the people involved. In particular, language will change between formal and informal communication. There are a number of reasons for this:

- In written communication, correct spelling, punctuation and grammar should be used in all types of business communication. Slang expressions, abbreviations and jargon should be avoided.

- Types of language might be more appropriate in some situations than others. For example, the language used between two friends is likely to be different from that used between a junior employee and a senior manager in an enterprise, which should show respect and a certain amount of deference. Language used between employees or colleagues on the same level of the organisational structure would be different again, reflecting their similar status.

- An employee should think about the language used when communicating with a customer or a prospective customer. The employee may be the 'first point of contact' and should make a good impression as this could be important in terms of sales and revenue. Formality and politeness without excessive use of jargon is best with customers; informality or being too personal may offend. Some enterprises may train their staff to use a particular style, and form of language, when dealing with customers.

- A representative of an enterprise would need to ensure that his or her language was appropriate for the context. For example, this would apply to the finance manager negotiating with a financial institution to provide a loan.

Verbal and non-verbal communication

Verbal communication is where messages are passed between people who are speaking to each other. This could involve a face-to-face conversation, a telephone conversation, a teleconference or a message left on a person's voicemail.

Non-verbal communication can be written, including letters, a memo or memorandum, email, report, form, notice board and information contained in a newspaper or a magazine.

Body language is where physical behaviour is used to express or convey feelings and thoughts. Examples include the use of postures, gestures and facial expressions.

Appropriateness of different types of communication for communicating with internal stakeholders

Stakeholders can be internal or external. Internal stakeholders are directly involved in the work of an enterprise, such as the managers, the employees, the shareholders and the owners.

Key terms

Body language: the process of communicating in a non-verbal way through conscious or unconscious gestures, movements and mannerisms

Verbal communication: messages between people in an enterprise that are spoken, such as in a face-to-face conversation

Written communication: messages between people in an enterprise that are written down in some way, such as in a letter

Written methods of communication with internal stakeholders

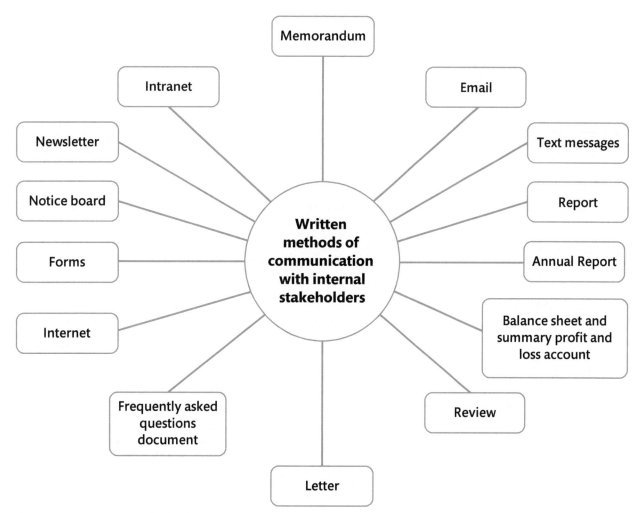

▲ **Figure 2** *Written methods of communication with internal stakeholders*

▲ **Figure 3** *An example of verbal communication*

▲ **Figure 4** *An Annual General Meeting in a company*

🔑 Key terms

Annual General Meeting: a yearly meeting of shareholders, which a limited company is usually legally required to hold

Horizontal communication: messages between people on the same organisational level of an enterprise

Intranet: a computer network that shares information resources and services within a particular enterprise

Vertical communication: messages between people on different organisational levels of an enterprise; there are two types of vertical communication – downwards and upwards

Verbal methods of communication with internal stakeholders

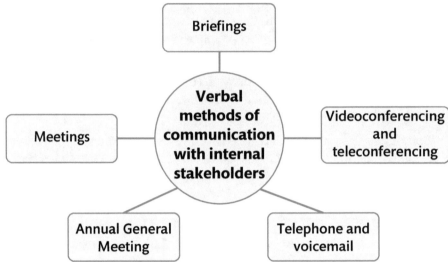

▲ **Figure 5** *Verbal methods of communication with internal stakeholders*

Appropriate methods of communication for different situations

- Memos, emails, text messages, briefings, meetings, a notice board, forms, a newsletter, the intranet, telephone and videoconferences are more likely to be used between managers and employees of an enterprise.

- Letters, reports, reviews, the frequently asked questions document and the internet can be used as methods of communication with shareholders as well as between managers and employees.

- The Annual Report, the balance sheet and summary profit and loss account and the Annual General Meeting are more likely to be used as methods of communicating with the shareholders of an enterprise.

Appropriateness of different types of communication for communicating with external stakeholders

External stakeholders are those that are not directly involved in the work of an enterprise, but are indirectly affected in various ways, such as suppliers, customers, financial institutions, the local community and local government.

Written methods of communication with external stakeholders

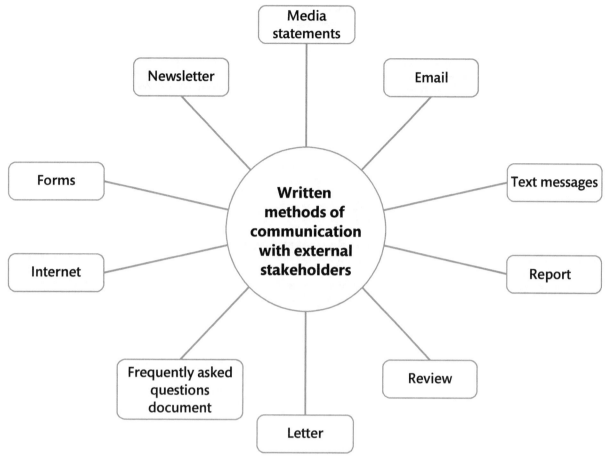

Verbal methods of communication with external stakeholders

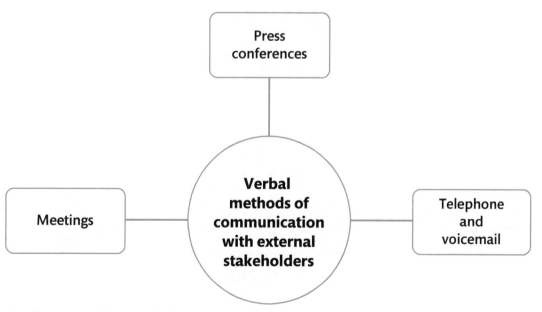

▲ **Figure 7** *Verbal methods of communication with external stakeholders*

Candidates sometimes confuse internal and external stakeholders. Make sure you understand the difference between them and that you can give examples of each.

Appropriate methods of communication for different situations

Some methods of communication are more appropriate for some situations than for others:

- Emails, text messages, letters, reviews, media statements, press conferences, the frequently asked questions document, the internet, forms, meetings and the telephone are likely to be used as methods of communication with suppliers, customers and local community organisations.

- A letter is more likely to be used as an initial method of communication with a government department, although further communication may be by email, text messages and telephone calls.

 Recap

- Methods of communication can be formal or informal depending on the audience.

- You need to recognise and provide examples of how and why language changes in formal and informal communication.

- You need to understand what both verbal and non-verbal communication are.

- You need to understand the appropriateness of different types of communication for communicating with internal and external stakeholders.

 Apply

Distinguish between formal and informal communication.

 Review

You must have a clear understanding of the different forms of communication that can be used not only within an enterprise but also when communicating with external stakeholders.

These different forms of communication can include formal and informal communication and also verbal and non-verbal communication.

Case studies can illustrate different forms of communication. Page 159 of the Student Book has a case study of the Debswana Diamond Company in Botswana, focusing on different forms of communication, such as meetings and press conferences, especially with local community organisations.

You need to know:

- the importance of being well planned, having a clear focus, keeping to time and ensuring that everyone has an opportunity to speak
- the importance of providing appropriate documents
- how to analyse and evaluate whether a meeting was successful and objectives were achieved.

Planning a meeting

If it is to be effective, a meeting needs to be well planned before, during and after. For example, all attendees need to know:

- where to arrive
- when to arrive
- what to bring.

The objective of a meeting

- *Clear focus*: for a meeting to achieve a desired outcome, it must be clear what the purpose or objective of a meeting actually is – a clear focus.

- *Clear objective*: a meeting should have a clear objective. For example, a meeting may have different possible objectives, which may conflict with each other. Once the objective of a meeting has been decided, it becomes possible to focus on this objective. This will influence the planning of the meeting and also help with the decisions about which people will be required to attend the meeting.

The use of time

A meeting needs to be planned so that it is possible to achieve the objective in the minimum of time – time is an important resource.

An agenda will need to be drawn up that makes it clear why the meeting is taking place, how participants should prepare and what they are expected to do at the meeting.

In the preparation of the agenda, a number of questions need to be asked:

- *Priorities*: what must be covered in the meeting?
- *Objective*: what is the fundamental aim or purpose of the meeting?
- *Participants*: who needs to attend the meeting?
- *Sequence*: in what order are the topics and issues to be covered?
- *Timing*: how much time needs to be spent on each topic or issue?
- *Date and time*: how much notice should be given of the meeting?
- *Place*: where will be the best place to hold the meeting?

A well thought-out agenda should help to keep a meeting focused on its objective so that time is not wasted. For example, if an agenda clearly shows how much time will be allocated to the discussion of a particular topic, and the allocated time is coming to an end, alternative strategies can be suggested instead of prolonging the length of the meeting. These could include the following:

- Set a deadline for the discussion in order to reach a decision within, say, the next five minutes.
- Defer the taking of a decision until another time.
- Delegate the taking of a decision to a separate sub-committee.

The use of an appropriate process at a meeting

Effective meetings need structure and order. There needs to be a clear agenda and a commitment to involve all of the participants:

- Some participants may dominate the discussion, so make sure everyone is invited to contribute to the discussions.

- At the end of each item on the agenda, quickly summarise what has been said and agreed. Ask the participants to confirm that they agree with the summary.

- Observe body language and consider what this may say about how the meeting is proceeding; for example, if the level of concentration of some participants is decreasing, it might be an appropriate time for a break.

- Ensure that the meeting stays on target in terms of going through the items on the agenda; irrelevance or digression needs to be avoided if time is to be used effectively.

- At the end of the meeting, quickly summarise what has been achieved and what action points have been agreed.

Documents for meetings and presentations

Notice of meeting

Those people who are required to attend a meeting need to be informed when and where the meeting will take place – by giving notice of a meeting. The notice of a meeting should not normally be given less than 7 days and not more than 21 days before the meeting is to be held.

Agenda

An agenda is a list of what is to be discussed at a meeting. It is circulated to the participants before a meeting takes place. This gives the participants the opportunity to prepare for the discussion and an indication of what to bring to the meeting.

The first three items of an agenda are always the same:

- *Apologies for absence*: from those people who are unable attend the meeting.

- *Minutes of the last meeting:* these are either read out or the participants are asked to refer to them.

- *Matters arising from the minutes*: the chairperson will ask if there are any points from the minutes that any participant feels the need to raise and discuss.

The last two items of an agenda are always the same:

- *Any other business*: this is the opportunity for the participants to raise any other issues that were not included on the agenda.

- *Date and time of next meeting*: a mutually convenient date and time for the next meeting is decided.

Key terms

Agenda: a list of items that will be discussed at a forthcoming meeting

Notice of meeting: the provision of information about the date, time and place of a forthcoming meeting

Minutes

There will be one designated person at the meeting, usually a secretary, who has the responsibility to take the minutes.

The minutes are circulated after a meeting has taken place. They can also indicate where action is required to be taken and by whom.

It is crucial that the minutes:

- are a true and accurate account of what took place at the meeting and of the decisions taken
- offer a brief summary of the main points discussed at the meeting
- offer a clear record of what took place at the meeting as they likely to be referred to in the future. They will also be read by those people who were unable to attend the meeting.

Visual aids

Software such as Microsoft PowerPoint® can be used to create slides that engage the participants' attention in a presentation, making use of motion, zoom and spatial relationships.

The advice on the production of slideshows is based on the 10–20–30 rule, where they should:

- contain no more than 10 slides
- last no more than 20 minutes
- use a font size of no less than 30 point.

Handouts

These are documents that support what is being covered in a presentation, usually to be taken away by the participants.

The benefits of handouts include the following:

- They cut down the amount of material covered in the presentation so that the presenter does not commit information overload.
- They allow the presenter not to worry about forgetting what to say.
- Members of the audience will have a concrete reminder making the presentation more memorable.
- Having handouts allows the audience members to concentrate on the presentation. They can make notes on the handouts if they wish.
- If the audience members are inspired by the presentation, they have information to hand on the topics covered.

Formal report

A formal report might be used to support a meeting or presentation. A formal report will involve a number of clear headings and subheadings where appropriate and it is usually divided into distinct sections. There are various types of formal reports, including problem-solving reports and feasibility studies.

▲ **Figure 8** *Clarification on the minutes of a meeting*

 Coursework tip

You will give a presentation as part of your enterprise project.

 Key terms

Formal report: a document that is written to provide information, analyse an issue and make recommendations

Minutes: a summary of what has taken place at a meeting

Exam tip

You need to be clear about how a formal report would be presented. It will usually be divided up into distinct sections, such as the following:

- title
- introduction
- findings
- conclusions
- tables, diagrams and appendices.

The effectiveness of meetings or presentations

It is important to consider how the effectiveness of a meeting or presentation can be evaluated. This involves asking three questions:

- Was the objective of the meeting or presentation achieved?
- Did the meeting or presentation take up a minimum amount of time?
- Did the participants at the meeting or presentation believe that an appropriate process had been followed?

Analysing and evaluating decisions made

One way to judge whether a meeting or presentation has been successful is to analyse and evaluate the decisions made there. An evaluation should focus on:

- the effectiveness of the speakers
- the participant experience – how much they learned
- the overall level of participant satisfaction as judged – was the presentation recommended by attendees and would they attend a similar meeting or presentation again.

Deciding if objectives were achieved

Judging how successfully the objectives of the meeting or presentation have been achieved could involve feedback from those present, using a questionnaire, which can then be analysed. The feedback may also include suggestions for improvement.

 Apply

Describe what is usually contained in the agenda of a meeting.

 **Review**

It is important to be able to judge the effectiveness of a meeting or a presentation, such as in relation to the decisions taken.

The case study of the enterprise the Leaf Group Company, on page 167 of the Student Book, has a step-by-step approach to the evaluation of a presentation so that it is possible to make a judgment as to whether a presentation was a success or not.

 Recap

There is a need for careful planning of meetings by:

- being well planned
- having a clear focus
- keeping to time
- ensuring everyone has an opportunity to speak.

It is important that documentation is produced, including:

- notice of meeting
- agenda
- minutes.

Documents for presentations include:

- visual aids
- handouts.

The success of a meeting or presentation can be determined by:

- analysing and evaluating decisions made
- deciding if objectives have been achieved.

Sample question

1. a. Define the term 'Annual General Meeting'. [2]

b. Explain, with the use of examples, the advantages of email as a method of communication between an enterprise and both internal and external stakeholders. [4]

c. Analyse why it is important that meetings should have a clear focus. [6]

d. Discuss why it is important to evaluate the success of meetings and presentations. [10]

Analysis

✓ In (a), you will need to clearly define what is meant by the term 'Annual General Meeting'.

✓ In (b), you will need to clearly explain the advantages of email as a method of communication between an enterprise and its stakeholders; you will need to refer to both internal and external stakeholders and you will need to include examples to support the explanation.

✓ In (c), you will need to analyse why it is important to the success of meetings that they should have a clear focus.

✓ In (d), you will need to provide a clear discussion of why it is important to evaluate the success of meetings and presentations once they have been completed.

Mark scheme

a. One mark for explaining that an Annual General Meeting is a meeting of shareholders that is held each year; one mark for explaining that it is something that a limited company is usually legally required to hold.

b. Up to two marks for an explanation of the advantages of email as a method of communication between an enterprise and its internal stakeholders; up to two marks for an explanation of the advantages of email as a method of communication between an enterprise and its external stakeholders. Appropriate examples should be used to support the explanation.

c. Up to six marks for an analysis of why it is important to the success of meetings that they should have a clear focus, especially in relation to the purpose and objective of the meeting.

d. Knowledge and understanding, Level 1, 1–3 marks; some analysis, Level 2, 4–7 marks; good analysis, Level 3, 8–10 marks.

Raise your grade

Student answer

(a) An Annual General Meeting, or AGM, is held each year in enterprises that are organised as a limited company. [1 mark]

(b) An email is a good form of communication between an enterprise and its stakeholders, especially where that communication is horizontal, i.e. between employees on the same level of the organisation structure. For example, reports and other documents can be sent as attachments to an email. An email can also be relatively informal. [2 marks]

(c) It is important that meetings should have a clear focus if they are to be successful and effective. They need to be planned thoroughly so that the participants understand what the objectives and aims of the meeting are. A clear focus will help to keep the participants attentive to what is being done at the meeting and this will improve the level of commitment and motivation. [3 marks]

(d) It is important to evaluate the success of meetings and presentations once they have been completed because lessons can be learned from what has taken place and appropriate changes made before the next meeting or presentation. This is especially the case in relation to the decisions made at a meeting or presentation. In the case of a presentation, the audience can be asked to complete a feedback questionnaire and the results can be analysed in terms of, for example, the effectiveness of the speakers, how much participants learned and also the overall level of participant satisfaction. [4 marks]

Total: 10 out of 22

 Examiner feedback

a. The candidate has correctly stated that an Annual General Meeting (AGM) is held each year in limited companies, but the definition could have been developed, e.g. by pointing out that an AGM is attended by the shareholders of a company and that its purpose is to give the shareholders the opportunity to express their views and opinions on the performance of the enterprise over the previous 12 months.

b. The candidate has explained the advantages of email as a method of communication between an enterprise and its internal stakeholders, but there is no reference to communication with external stakeholders. Many enterprises now use email for communicating with external stakeholders on a regular basis. For example, the marketing department will often use email to communicate with customers, to make them aware of special offers or of new products. Email is also likely to be used between an enterprise and its suppliers, e.g. for confirming in writing what has been agreed over the telephone.

c. The candidate has made an attempt to analyse why it is important that meetings should have a clear focus, but the answer could have been developed more fully. For example, there could have been a reference to a clear focus helping the participants to generate different, but appropriate and logical, ideas or to it helping the participants set out a plan to achieve the agreed objectives.

d. The candidate has made a reasonable attempt to suggest why it is important to evaluate the success of meetings and presentations, but the answer could have been expanded upon, especially in relation to the issue of whether the objectives of the meeting or presentation were actually achieved. Any meeting or presentation will have particular objectives that it will seek to achieve and so the evaluation of whether such objectives have been achieved will be important. For example, consideration of the responses of the feedback questionnaires could be widened to include suggestions for improvement.

Unit 11:
Coursework

Component 2 is the coursework and makes up 50% of the total marks.

Tick these boxes to build a record of your revision

Specification	Theme	Tick
11.1 Choosing a suitable project	Coursework suggestions	
	Practical considerations	
11.2 Task 1 Explaining your choice of project	The formal written report	
11.3 Task 2 Planning the project	Task 2a Action plan	
	Task 2b Option 1: Planning for financing the project	
	Task 2b Option 2: Planning marketing communications	
11.4 Task 3 Using enterprise skills to implement the plan	A written record of how five enterprise skills were used	
11.5 Task 4 Evaluating the project	The formal written report	
	Checklist of coursework evidence	

You need to know:

• what deliberation needs to go into choosing your enterprise project.

Component 2: Coursework involves a portfolio of evidence based on an enterprise project that you must plan and run. You should not simply choose the first idea you think of. Instead, a great deal of deliberation needs to go into choosing one, rather than another, enterprise project.

Coursework suggestions

You should carry out an enterprise project, either on your own or as a member of a group of usually not more than six people.

Learners working alone

If you work on your own, you will take sole responsibility for carrying out a relatively small and simple project, such as:

• gardening, grass cutting or tidying up a yard

• pet sitting, dog walking or any similar activities involving caring for an animal

• baby sitting

• car washing or valeting

• tutoring younger students or helping them with different aspects of their learning

• making and selling small items, such as jewellery, flower baskets, picture frames or wooden ornaments

• small-scale local community and environmental projects, such as in relation to recycling used materials.

Learners working in groups

If you are working in a group, you should carry out a larger and more complex project. This will allow each member of the group to play and demonstrate a separate, defined role. Possible projects could include:

• providing a snack shop or a similar catering facility in a school or college

• recycling clothes

• producing candles, party decorations or calendars

• staging an event, such as a fashion show, an exhibition or a sporting event

• organising and running a trip or visit for other students

• organising a market stall or exhibition at a trade fair

• producing cushions, bird boxes or printed T-shirts

• repairing and servicing bicycles

• local community projects: an environmental project would be ideal for a social enterprise project.

Practical considerations

The choice of project will depend upon such factors as:

• the range of facilities and resources available to learners

• the skills, attributes, interests, talents and experience of learners

• the amount of time available to carry out the activity or project

• whether you will work alone or as part of a group.

In order to produce evidence in each of the four tasks of the coursework, it is important that opportunities should be given to:

• plan the project and monitor progress

• obtain the necessary finance

• communicate with potential customers

• negotiate with another person or with a group of people.

You need to know:

- how to present appropriate evidence that you have evaluated a number of possible enterprise projects before making your final choice.

The formal written report

In this task, you are required to produce a formal written report that considers two or three ideas for possible projects and to give a detailed explanation for your choice of project.

In the formal written report, you will need to:

- outline and analyse the advantages and disadvantages of each idea
- collect, present and analyse appropriate data
- give a detailed explanation of the reasons for the choice of project and a justified decision, including why other ideas were rejected
- write in a formal report style.

The advantages and disadvantages of each idea

The report will need to include a number of advantages and disadvantages of each enterprise idea. This will include not only the idea chosen but also those that were discarded.

The inclusion of relevant data

You will need to collect, present and analyse appropriate data for each possible idea. Data could be presented by using the results of market research or in the form of a SWOT or PEST analysis.

Reasons for the choice of project

You will need to give a detailed explanation of the reasons for the choice of enterprise project. You also need to include a summary of the reasons why other ideas were rejected. In this part of the report, you will need to make clear why you chose one project rather than another, outlining the main reasons for your choice.

Formal report

A formal report should include:

- headings
- subheadings
- charts
- tables
- diagrams
- clear links to appendices, where appropriate.

The report has an approximate word count of 1200 words, excluding charts, tables, diagrams and appendices. This should give you the flexibility to explore two or three options and to give an explanation of your final choice of enterprise project.

Coursework tip

You should produce the formal written report before you begin your chosen enterprise project.

Common error

Make sure you remember to give an outline of how the particular enterprise project was chosen AND why other possibilities were not chosen.

Common error

Candidates sometimes produce a formal written report in Task 1 that is too short. You should aim to produce a report of approximately 1200 words, excluding charts, tables, diagrams and appendices.

Coursework tip

The word count is designed to encourage depth, rather than breadth, of analysis.

You need to know:

- how to use an action plan to plan a project and manage potential problems
- how to plan to finance the project
  OR
- how to plan marketing communications.

Task 2 is divided into two parts. Task 2a is on planning to manage potential problems or issues in the action plan. Task 2b is on planning for financing the project OR on planning marketing communication.

Task 2a Action plan

You are required to produce an action plan. The answers to the following questions form the six stages of an action plan:

- *What are the key activities or tasks?* It should be made clear exactly what the enterprise intends to do and how these activities or tasks are to be carried out.

- *When must the key activities or tasks take place, and how long will they take?* The action plan needs to make it very clear not only what is happening in the enterprise, but also how long the various activities or tasks are likely to take and when they will take place. Tasks should have realistic timescales.

- *Who is responsible for carrying out the key activities or tasks?* The action plan needs to be very precise about who is doing what in the enterprise, making it clear who has responsibility for various tasks or activities.

- *By what date does each key activity or task need to be completed?* The action plan must make clear the agreed dates for the completion of the activities or tasks. The enterprise needs to draw up a timetable that summarises the key dates by which time certain activities or tasks have to be completed.

- *How will progress be monitored?* It is important to consider how the tasks in the action plan are regularly checked so that what is supposed to be happening in the enterprise is actually happening – effective monitoring of progress is vitally important to the eventual success of an enterprise.

- *What was the outcome (after key activities are completed)?* An action plan should include information about the eventual outcome of the activities or tasks, however successful or unsuccessful these were.

Managing potential problems or issues in the action plan

You will use the action plan to identify key activities within the enterprise project. If the action plan is agreed in a group, the significant activities identified must be your own individual choices. For this task, you should:

- identify two or three significant activities from the action plan for your enterprise project

- identify potential problems or issues for each activity and describe how you plan to manage each problem or issue

- submit a written analysis of potential problems or issues and how you intend to manage them.

▲ **Figure 1** *Putting together an action plan for an enterprise project*

> **Coursework tip**
>
> You should produce the action plan before you begin your chosen enterprise project.

> **Coursework tip**
>
> Don't forgot that in addition to the identification of potential problems, you need to identify solutions for two or three activities.

> **Coursework tip**
>
> You must submit the action plan, but the plan will not be assessed.

Task 2b Option 1: Planning for financing the project

Task 2b requires you to provide written evidence of one of the following options:

- planning for financing the project

OR

- planning for marketing communications.

You must give a presentation of your proposals for the chosen option, demonstrating your communication and enterprise skills.

Written evidence of the sources of finance

You need to research three or four appropriate sources of finance for the enterprise project. The written evidence will consist of the following financial aspects:

- the various sources of finance that you considered for the different financial needs of the project

- your decision on which source(s) to use

- an explanation of why you believe that you have chosen the best and most appropriate source(s) for the project.

The evidence is likely to contain information in relation to the following five aspects:

- the costs of materials and equipment

- the potential methods of finance available

- the advantages and disadvantages of different sources of finance

- the method(s) of finance chosen.

If you are working in a group, you may create a budget together. Individual or group budgets may be submitted as an appendix for reference.

Witness statement of a presentation (finance)

For both options of Task 2b, you also need to submit a witness statement, which will comment on your communication and enterprise skills, while making a presentation. The presentation should be to a teacher or to a business person and it should include the use of visual materials. The presentation should cover your proposals and reasons for the choice(s) of finance.

In addition to the witness statement, it would also be helpful if the script and any visual material used for the presentation were included. The witness statement is likely to include:

- your name

- the type of event

- the date of the event

- the size of the audience at the presentation

- how you demonstrated listening skills

- how well you interacted with the audience

- your skills development

- the initiative you showed and the problem-solving skills you demonstrated.

 Coursework tip

Individual or group budgets may be submitted but these will not be assessed.

Task 2b Option 2: Planning marketing communications

Task 2b requires you to provide one of the following options:

* written evidence of planning for marketing communications

OR

* planning for financing the project.

You must give a presentation of your proposals for the chosen option, demonstrating your communication and enterprise skills.

Written evidence of types of marketing communications

The written evidence will consist of three aspects of the enterprise:

* the types of marketing communication you considered
* your decision on which method(s) to use
* an explanation of why you believe your chosen method(s) will be successful.

Different examples of marketing communication are:

* poster
* leaflet
* design plan for a website
* story board for a television advertisement
* written script for a radio advertisement
* sponsorship materials.

A written description or script of a radio or television advertisement, or a story board showing the ideas for the advertisement will be sufficient.

Witness statement of a presentation (marketing)

You will also need to submit a witness statement, which will comment on your communication and enterprise skills, while making a presentation.

The presentation should be to a teacher or to a business person and it should include the use of visual materials. The presentation should cover your proposed methods of marketing communications and your reasons for the choice of communications.

In addition to the witness statement, it would also be helpful if the script and any visual material used for the presentation was included. As with the presentation on financial planning, you need to ensure that the presentation is appropriate for the audience and that it is communicated as effectively and as clearly as possible.

If you are working in a group, you may create examples of marketing communications together. Individual or group examples of marketing communications may be submitted as an appendix for reference.

Coursework tip

Individual or group examples of marketing communications may be submitted but these will not be assessed.

You need to know:
- how to submit a written record of how you used five enterprise skills in your enterprise project
- how to carry out an individual plan for negotiation.

A written record of how five enterprise skills were used

Entrepreneurial skills were considered in Unit 3, when it was pointed out that you would need to be able to identify and evaluate your own skills during your enterprise project.

Task 3 requires you to identify five of your own enterprise skills from those in Unit 3.1, evaluate these skills and explain how you demonstrated them during the enterprise project. One of these skills must be negotiation.

You will need to submit a written record of how you used the five named skills to implement your enterprise project. You must only write about your own skills.

Individual plan for a negotiation

You must also plan and conduct a negotiation with someone outside the enterprise project team to secure support for an aspect of the project.

This individual plan for a negotiation must include details of:

- the people involved in the negotiation
- the situation of the negotiation
- the benefits and weaknesses of your proposal
- the outcomes of the negotiation.

During the course of the enterprise project, you will have been involved in a number of different possible negotiating situations. For example, this could be negotiation with a representative of a financial institution in order to arrange finance, or negotiation to rent equipment or to pay for a market stall.

In the individual plan for a negotiation, you need to:

- make clear exactly who was involved in the negotiation and what each person's role in the process was
- state where and when the negotiation took place
- summarise the essential advantages and limitations of what was being discussed in the negotiation.
- provide details of the outcome of the negotiation, e.g. was a degree of compromise necessary?

 Coursework tip

One of the five enterprise skills MUST be negotiation. The other four skills can be from the following:

- the practical skills and knowledge to create products
- leadership
- influencing skills
- team-building
- delegation
- problem-solving
- prioritisation and management
- self-confidence
- resourcefulness
- innovation
- taking initiative
- taking calculated risks
- taking responsibility
- motivation and a determination to succeed
- creativity and perseverance.

You need to know:
- how to evaluate all aspects of a project.

Coursework tip

The choice of the internal communications option is only available if you have been working in a group.

Coursework tip

You should focus on how well your plans were implemented, not on evaluating your own performance.

Coursework tip

The word count is designed to encourage depth, rather than breadth, of analysis.

Common error

Candidates sometimes produce a formal written report in Task 4 that is too short. You should aim to produce a report of approximately 1500 words, excluding charts, tables, diagrams and appendices.

The formal written report

Task 4 requires you to produce a formal written report. In this report, firstly you will analyse and evaluate the planning and implementation of the project. Secondly, you will analyse and evaluate ONE from the financing of the project, the marketing communications used or the internal communications used (this option is only available if you are working as part of a group).

The evaluation of the planning and implementation of the project

This part of Task 4 requires you to analyse and evaluate your project and make recommendations for improvement in areas such as:

- the methods used to plan the enterprise project
- any deviations from the plan
- how well the plan was implemented.

The evaluation of the financing of the project

The areas for analysis and evaluation could include:

- the suitability of the sources of finance used
- the way income and expenditure were managed and monitored
- the extent to which the project achieved its financial aims.

The evaluation of the marketing communications used

The areas for analysis and evaluation could include:

- the suitability of marketing communications used in terms of cost
- the appropriateness of the marketing communications used
- how well the marketing communication methods used helped to attract potential customers.

The evaluation of the internal communications used

The areas for analysis and evaluation could include:

- the suitability of the channels used
- the flow, speed and accuracy of communication achieved.

The content of the formal written report

In the report, you need to:

- analyse and evaluate positive and negative outcomes for each chosen area
- explain differences between predictions and actual events
- use evidence to support the points made
- give clear and reasoned recommendations for improvement for each area
- write in a formal report style.

The task has an approximate word count of 1500 words, excluding charts, tables, diagrams and appendices. The approximate word count, excluding charts, tables, diagrams and appendices, is designed to give you the flexibility to explore the positive and negative outcomes of two areas.

Checklist of coursework evidence

Task	You must submit	Tick
1	A formal written report of approximately 1200 words on identifying an appropriate enterprise project.	
2a	An action plan (for reference). Identification of potential problems and solutions for two or three activities.	
2b	**EITHER** Planning for financing the project: • written evidence of the sources of finance you considered. • presentation witness statement. **OR** Planning marketing communications: • written evidence of the types of marketing communication you considered. • presentation witness statement.	
3	A written description of how five enterprise skills (from Unit 3.1 of the subject content) were used. A plan for negotiation.	
4	A formal written report of approximately 1500 words including: • the planning and implementation of the project and **ONE** of the following: • the financing of the project • the marketing communication used • the internal communications used (this option is only available if you were working in a group).	

Glossary

Action plan a plan that outlines the actions required to achieve particular aims and objectives and which provides a way of monitoring progress

Agenda a list of items that will be discussed at a forthcoming meeting

Aim an overall general goal that an enterprise wants to achieve in the long term

Announcement a public and typically formal statement about a particular occurrence or intention

Annual General Meeting a yearly meeting of shareholders, which a limited company is usually legally required to hold

Body language the process of communicating in a non-verbal way through conscious or unconscious gestures, movements and mannerisms

Brand a name or image that clearly distinguishes one product from another

Brand loyalty the degree to which consumers buy a particular brand of a product in preference to another brand

Branding the strategy of differentiating the products of one enterprise from those of another through emphasising an identifiable image

Break-even the break-even point is when the total revenue of an enterprise exactly matches the total costs and the enterprise is not making either a profit or a loss

Budget a financial statement of income and expenditure prior to a particular period of time

Budget variance the difference between a budgeted or anticipated figure and the actual figure

Building society a financial institution that receives deposits and provides loans and other forms of financial support. It is usually owned by its members, and so is a mutual organisation

Business and enterprise network a means of bringing together people to share, and learn from, their experiences in business and enterprise

Business enterprise a type of enterprise that usually has profit as its main objective

Business organisation an organisation that has been established with the purpose of producing and selling particular goods and services

Business plan a document that summarises the main aims and objectives of an enterprise and how these aims and objectives are to be achieved

Cash flow the inflow of money into and the outflow of money out of an enterprise

Cash flow forecast a forecast of expected income and expenditure over a particular period of time

Cash inflows cash flowing into an enterprise as receipts, e.g. from the money received from selling goods or services

Cash outflows cash flowing out of an enterprise as payments, e.g. to pay employees and suppliers

Commercial bank a commercial institution that receives deposits and provides loans and other forms of financial support. It is usually owned by its shareholders

Consultant a person who provides expert advice in a particular area of enterprise activity

Consumer sovereignty the importance of changes in consumer preferences in determining the allocation of scarce resources in an economy

Contribution the difference between sales revenue and variable costs

Co-operative a type of business organisation owned by its customers or its employees

Corporate social responsibility the willingness of an enterprise to accept responsibility for its actions and how they may impact on a variety of stakeholders

Creative the ability to introduce something original and imaginative

Credit a sum of money that a supplier allows an entrepreneur before requiring payment and/or a sum of money that an enterprise allows a customer before requiring payment

Credit union a financial institution that receives deposits and provides loans and other forms of financial support. It is usually owned by its members, and so is a mutual organisation, but it tends to be limited to particular areas of a country or to particular groups of workers

Creditor a person or organisation that is owed money

Crowdfunding the practice of funding an enterprise project or venture by raising small amounts of money from a large number of people, typically via the internet

Customer a person or organisation that buys products from an enterprise

Customer retention the degree to which customers are loyal to an enterprise and are likely to buy its products again in the future

Customer satisfaction the degree to which the products supplied by an enterprise, and the quality of the service provided in selling those products, meet or exceed the expectations of customers

Debt a sum of money that is owed by a person or organisation

Debtor a person or organisation that owes money

Deficit the amount by which an enterprise's expenditure or spending exceeds its income over a particular period of time

Delegation where responsibility is passed down to others in an enterprise

Desk research the ways of gaining second-hand information through such methods as analysing sales figures from inside an enterprise or using government research reports from outside the enterprise

Dividend a share of the profit of an enterprise in the form of a payment to its shareholders

Enterprise a business organised and run by an entrepreneur

Enterprise process the six stages that are involved in the setting up of a new enterprise

Enterprising the showing of initiative, imagination, energy and resourcefulness

Entrepreneur the person in an enterprise who makes decisions and takes and manages risks

Equity see Share

Ethical principle a way of doing something according to a set of moral principles, values and beliefs

External sources of finance funds that are found outside an enterprise

Expenditure or **spending** all of the outgoings of an enterprise over a specific period of time

Field research ways of gaining first-hand information through such methods as a questionnaire or an interview

Finance the activities of an enterprise that are related to money

Fixed costs the costs of an enterprise that do not vary directly with changes in the level of output

Focus group a small number of people who are brought together to give feedback on a specific good or service

Formal communication the official channels of communication used within an enterprise

Formal report a document that is written to provide information, analyse an issue and make recommendations

Franchise an arrangement whereby one company gives the right to an enterprise to supply its products

Franchisee the enterprise allowed by a company to conduct business using that company's name and brand

Franchisor the company that allows the enterprise to conduct business using its name and brand

Friendly society a financial institution that receives deposits and provides loans and other forms of financial support. It is usually owned by its members, and so is a mutual organisation. It is similar to a building society, but tends to be on a smaller scale, specialising in providing savings accounts and life insurance plans

Globalisation the trend towards worldwide markets in goods and services

Grant a payment that is usually given to support a particular project or service

Gross profit the sales revenue of an enterprise less the cost of sales

Growth the increase in size of an enterprise through internal and/or external expansion

Horizontal communication messages between people on the same organisational level of an enterprise

Income all of the incomings of an enterprise received from different sources over a specific period of time

Income statement or **profit and loss account** a statement that shows the net profit of an enterprise after all of the expenses have been deducted

Incorporated enterprise an enterprise that has a separate legal identity from the owner

Incubation centre a place where resources, space and an appropriate environment are provided for entrepreneurs to start up an enterprise

Informal communication the unofficial channels of communication used within an enterprise

Innovate the ability to introduce something new or different

Innovation the process of putting a new idea into practice

Interest the return on money that has been lent or the payment for money that has been borrowed

Internal sources of finance funds that are obtained within an enterprise

Internet a global system of interconnected computer networks that provides an extensive range of information resources and services

Intranet a computer network that shares information resources and services within a particular enterprise

Leadership style the distinctive way in which decisions are taken in an enterprise

Lease a contractual arrangement whereby an asset is used for a specified period of time on payment of rent

Legal compliance the process or procedure to ensure that an enterprise follows relevant laws, rules and regulations

Lessee the person or organisation that rents an asset from a lessor

Lessor the person or organisation that rents out an asset to a lessee

Limited company a company that is legally independent from its shareholders, who as a result have limited liability

Limited liability legal protection that allows shareholders to be liable for company debts only up to the value of their shareholding

Liquidity the ease with which the assets of an enterprise can be turned into cash

Loan money that is lent by a financial institution to a borrower

Loss the gap or shortfall between an enterprise's sales revenues and the total costs incurred in producing the output of the enterprise

Market orientation an approach where an enterprise takes decisions on the basis of consumer demand

Market research the collection and analysis of information that relates to the consumption of goods or services

Marketing the process of communicating relevant information in order to influence the behaviour of consumers in ways that will benefit an enterprise

Marketing strategy a long-term plan devised in order to achieve particular marketing objectives

Mass media a mixture of various technologies that are used to reach an audience

Mentor an experienced person who will be a source of useful advice

Minutes a summary of what has taken place at a meeting

Mortgage a form of loan that is usually secured against a property

Mystery shopper a person employed by a market research firm to visit retail establishments, posing as a casual shopper, to collect information on products and the quality of service

Need an item that is essential for survival

Negotiating style a particular approach to the process of negotiation

Negotiation an interaction of influences that aims to reach an outcome that will satisfy the interests of those involved

Net cash flow the difference between money coming into and out of an enterprise; it can either be a surplus or a deficit

Net profit the gross profit of an enterprise less all other expenses

Notice of meeting the provision of information about the date, time and place of a forthcoming meeting

Objective a specific target than an enterprise wants to achieve in the short term

Organisational structure the particular way in which an enterprise is structured in order to perform its different activities

Overdraft a situation when an account is allowed to go into debit

Partnership a type of business organisation that is owned by two or more people

Perseverance the determination and persistence to achieve something despite experiencing difficulties

PEST analysis the analysis of the wider macro-environment of an enterprise, including *political, economic, social* and *technological* factors

Positive attitude the tendency to be optimistic

Pressure group an organisation that aims to influence governments and enterprises to adopt policies and actions it favours

Primary research the collection of information that does not already exist through different forms of field research

Product life cycle the typical sales pattern of a product over time from its introduction in a market to its eventual decline

Profit the difference between the total revenue and the total cost of an enterprise

Profit and loss account see Income statement

Profit maximisation the goal of many enterprises to make the gap between total revenue and total cost as wide as possible

Qualitative research the gaining of information in the form of soft subjective data, e.g. opinions and attitudes

Quantitative research the gaining of information in the form of hard objective data, e.g. statistics

Real income the increase in income after subtracting the rate of inflation

Regional policy a government policy that is designed to concentrate help and support in particular areas of a country

Revenue the income received from the sales of goods and/or services of an enterprise over a specific period of time

Risk the possibility that events in relation to an enterprise do not turn out as expected

Risk-averse an attitude to risk characterised by being unwilling or disinclined to take any risk

Risk-keen an attitude to risk based on recognition that a high level of risk is likely to lead to a high level of profit

Risk reducer a person who wishes to reduce the amount of risk faced by an enterprise to reduce the likelihood of failure

Sales revenue maximisation where an enterprise aims to maximise the revenue received from sales rather than its profit

Satisficing where an enterprise aims for an adequate level of profit, rather than profit maximisation

Secondary research the collection of information that already exists through different forms of desk research

Share or equity a contribution to the finance needed by an enterprise organised as a limited company; a share certificate is issued to the shareholder

Shareholder an individual who contributes funds to a limited company in return for shares in the company

SMART objectives or **targets** objectives or targets that are *specific, measurable, achievable, realistic* and *time based*

Social enterprise a type of enterprise that does not usually have profit as its main objective

Social impact of enterprise the impact, either positive or negative, that an enterprise may have on communities and society

Social media websites, other online means of communication and applications that enable users to share information and to participate in social networking

Social responsibility the idea that an enterprise has a responsibility towards the wider society and environment

Sole trader a person responsible for setting up and running an enterprise that he or she runs alone

Solvency the degree to which the current assets of an enterprise are greater than its current liabilities

Spending see Expenditure

Sponsorship a situation where an enterprise supports an event or an organisation in some way and receives publicity as a result

Stakeholders various groups with a strong interest in a particular enterprise, including customers and consumers, employees and employers, suppliers, lenders, the local business community and local government

Start-up the beginning of an enterprise when it is first established

Subsidy a payment that is usually given to keep the price charged to a consumer lower than would otherwise be the case

Suppliers businesses providing resources to an enterprise that allows it to produce goods and services

Glossary

Surplus the amount by which an enterprise's income exceeds its expenditure or spending over a particular period of time

SWOT analysis an acronym for *strengths*, *weaknesses*, *opportunities* and *threats*; it is a structured planning method that evaluates these four elements of an enterprise

Target audience a particular group of people who are identified as the intended recipient of an advertisement or message

Team-building the process of improving the effectiveness and motivation of people working together in a team

Technology the use of tools, machines and science in the production of goods

Total costs the total costs of an enterprise are made up of variable costs and fixed costs

Trade credit the credit extended by a seller to the purchaser of goods and services

Trade payables money owed by an enterprise to suppliers

Trade receivables money owed by customers to an enterprise

Unincorporated enterprise an enterprise that does not have a separate legal identity from the owner

Unique selling point (USP) a feature of a product that makes it different from other similar products, and therefore more attractive to people who might buy it

Unlimited liability the need for sole traders and partners (except limited partners) to pay the debts of an enterprise out of their own personal funds

Variable costs the costs of an enterprise that vary directly with changes in the level of output

Venture capital a collective investment scheme designed to provide private equity capital for relatively small expanding enterprises

Verbal communication messages between people in an enterprise that are spoken, such as in a face-to-face conversation

Vertical communication messages between people on different organisational levels of an enterprise; there are two types of vertical communication – downwards and upwards

Want an item that is desirable, but not essential

Website a set of web pages served from a single web domain; all publicly accessible websites collectively comprise the World Wide Web

Word of mouth people speaking to each other about a particular enterprise

Working capital the finance required by an enterprise to pay for the costs of production until payment is received for the output that has been produced

Written communication messages between people in an enterprise that are written down in some way, such as in a letter